Hollywood
'1970s

Hollywood 1970s

David Castell

GALLERY BOOKS

This book was devised and produced by
Multimedia Publications (UK) Ltd

Editor: Richard Rosenfeld
Assistant Editor: Dan Millar
Production: Karen Bromley
Design: Mick Hodson
Picture Research: David Sutherland

First published in the United States of America 1986 by Gallery
Books, an imprint of W.H. Smith Publishers Inc., 112 Madison
Avenue, New York, NY 10016

ISBN 0 8317 4524 X

Typeset by Letterspace Limited
Origination by Imago
Printed in Italy by Sagdos, Milan

Contents

Endpapers: *Warren Beatty was producer, cowriter, director and star of **Heaven Can Wait** (1978), a witty remake of the 1941 comedy **Here Comes Mr Jordan**. In this version Beatty is a footballer sent prematurely to a celestial rendezvous (by Concorde) but, since his own body has already been cremated, he is forced to mark time in the earthly shell of another man, a prime candidate for murder.*

Page 1: *Clint Eastwood played a bare-knuckle fistfighter in **Every Which Way But Loose** (1978) and **Any Which Way You Can** (1980).*

Page 2: *Thanks to intelligent and craftsmanlike performances by Dustin Hoffman and Meryl Streep, Robert Benton's **Kramer vs Kramer** (1979) transcended all expectations of tearjerking sentimentality as a study of the collapse of a marriage and the ensuing tug-of-love for custody of the only child (Justin Henry). Having left her husband and son, the wife later returns, hoping to regain her child's affection.*

This page: *One of the many remarkable, surrealistic production numbers in Bob Fosse's **All That Jazz** (1979).*

Tombstone California

Chapter 1

I n the late Fifties the prescient wise men of the motion picture business realized that Hollywood, as both the spiritual capital of the movies and the geographical hub of the industry, was entering its twilight years.

Ben Hecht's 1957 prophecy that, before the end of the century, Hollywood would be "just another tourist spot like Tombstone, Arizona," is already well on thé way to being fulfilled. I made my first and only visit there in 1985 when, of sixteen interviews that had been arranged, only one took place in a working studio (and that with an actor-producer preparing a project that has still to come to fruition). Everyone else was working from home, from independent production offices or on location.

At Universal the tourists are not only catered for but actively wooed. Their celebrated studio tour (which earns enough each year by way of admissions to finance two modest feature films) is a glum monument to a vanished age. Not that it isn't modest fun when Bruce, the killer shark from Steven Spielberg's **Jaws** (1975) lurches out of a lake at the tourists. But the film itself was very properly shot at sea, and the stranding even of a mechanical relic in a studio tank has undertones of zoological indignity.

Mementos of studio-made pictures are few, for the age that many insist on calling golden slips deeper and deeper into the past. The Victorian-Gothic mansion from which Anthony Perkins once looked down at the Bates motel in Alfred Hitchcock's **Psycho** (1960) stands gaunt against the Californian haze, but so much of the mystique of film-making is now deliberately exploded by behind-the-scenes documentaries that nobody is much surprised when the relentlessly cheerful tour guide exposes the trickery.

"You see, this building is just a facade," she explains, adding thoughtfully that, "facade is a French word meaning false front." And Hollywood, of course, built its reputation on being the American word for false front. The dream factories of Warners and Columbia, Paramount and Universal, MGM, 20th Century-Fox and others now forgotten by all but devotees of late-night movies peddled their wares for decades with only internal hiccups to disturb them. But the advent of television and its bushfire spread through the consumer world in the Fifties was to be a delayed trauma for the motion picture industry.

Producer David O. Selznick summed up the size of the threat to the film-making Establishment while he was supervising the location filming of his ill-fated **A Farewell to Arms** (1957). "Hollywood is like Egypt, full of crumbling pyramids," he said. "It will never come back; it will just keep crumbling until the wind blows the last studio props across the sand."

Right: *Jack Nicholson gave an eye-catching performance in Bob Rafelson's **Five Easy Pieces** (1970) as a middle-class drifter who cuts loose from family ties, finding more vitality in working-class company while still retaining his snobbish sense of superiority.*

Selznick's wind of change was then already groaning in the rigging and stirring the sails of Hollywood, but the studios resolutely declined to change course. They had control of the way a film looked, by dint of the four-wall imprisonment within their sound stages; they had control of the way it sounded, by dint of a voluntary pre-censorship that, even in the mid-Sixties, was offering under the guise of risqué sex comedies countless variations on the theme of the middle-aged virgin pursued by playful middle-aged bachelors who packed a wedding ring as surely as the Ringo Kid carried a rifle.

So the major companies simply marked time, doing what they had always done, but doing it more expensively and with less commercial success. Financial contraction meant that they made economies, often in the areas in which expenditure was most prudent (script development, the training of the young actors and actresses who had been put under contract for their looks rather than any natural acting abilities). A side-effect of this last measure was that, while contract artists of the Fifties such as Rock Hudson and Robert Wagner went on to become household names and box-office champions, new projects had to rely on the interest of one of no more than a dozen top stars on whose name and track record finance could be raised. Many a script, like that of **Butch Cassidy and the Sundance Kid** (1969), arrived at its final destination dog-eared and marked with the fingerprints of other major stars who had turned it down.

Bottom left: Mike Nichols' **Carnal Knowledge** (1971), scripted by Jules Feiffer, broke sexual taboos in the frankness with which it tackled its study of two college room-mates and the changes in their sexual attitudes. The action spanned their schooldays in the late Forties up to middle-age in the early Seventies. Jack Nicholson was the lawyer who has a stormy relationship with his mistress (Ann-Margret); Art Garfunkel and Candice Bergen played the couple who opt for marriage.

Below: People wept while standing in line to see **Love Story** (1970), Arthur Hiller's maudlin tale (taken from Erich Segal's tearful bestseller) of a dislikable preppie (Ryan O'Neal) who marries the lower-class fellow student (Ali MacGraw) who is dying of cancer. The weepie of the decade; astonishingly popular worldwide.

Hollywood rebels

No single film caused the change of attitudes that liberated the new Hollywood in the Seventies, but the one that struck the loudest contemporary chord was **Easy Rider** (1969). Independently made, outspoken in its theme, its language and its violence, it never saw the inside of a studio. But it touched a nerve with young audiences throughout the world, and its profit-to-cost ratio excited the studio heads.

The story of a journey across America by two drug-dealing drop-outs, **Easy Rider** was the brainchild of two celebrated Hollywood rebels, Peter Fonda and Dennis Hopper. The latter had fallen out with the film-making Establishment because off-screen he resembled too closely his on-screen persona of James Dean's delinquent enemy in **Rebel Without a Cause** (1955); Peter was the youngest of the feuding Fondas, and had begun the decade as a Brilliantined intern opposite Sandra Dee in **Tammy and the Doctor** (1963). Together they brought fresh images of young people to the screen and helped to bring a new audience to the cinema. More than any other single film **Easy Rider** altered our perception and expectations of the Hollywood cinema.

The Seventies marked the polarization of that cinema. It had to cater for an ever younger audience. Driven by hard necessity to offer

Top far left: *The film that changed it all: Dennis Hopper's* **Easy Rider** *(1969), produced by Peter Fonda and starring the two Hollywood rebels in a bike-road-and-drugs movie that altered all the rules in an industry suffering from financial elephantiasis. Its exclusive use of location filming and contemporary music on the soundtrack made it a surprise box-office hit.*

Bottom left: *In* **Marathon Man** *(1976), Dustin Hoffman tracks down the ex-concentration camp "doctor" (played by Laurence Olivier) who has recently murdered his secret-agent brother (played by Roy Scheider). Hoffman forces the old man to eat some of his hoard of diamonds before shooting him dead. Written by William Goldman and directed by John Schlesinger.*

Below: *In* **Five Easy Pieces** *(1970), Bobby Eroica Dupea (Jack Nicholson) rejects his upper-crust, musically talented family, preferring beer and sex among the "redneck crackers" of the Southern oilfields. But when he is unable to prevent his best friend from being beaten up by gangsterlike thugs (who are actually policemen and assault him too) and then hauled off to prison, he is disillusioned and returns (briefly) to the bosom of his family, symbolically located on a luxurious island near Seattle.*

something that television could not, it had to resort to extremes of violence, language and sexual behavior. And, as the studios slipped from the control of film-sated tycoons and into the hands of conglomerates and multinationals, that polarization extended to finance as well as content.

Those who wanted a nice little profit from a safe little movie found that the film world had progressed without them. The gap between success and failure was a yawning chasm into which many took a fatal tumble, and a Las Vegas gaming table mentality swept the cinema. Stars were paid bigger and bigger salaries (Marlon Brando earned a sum in excess of $4 million plus 11.3 percent of the profits of **Superman the Movie** (1978) in exchange for just twelve days' work) to lure larger and larger audiences. It wasn't so much that fewer people were going to the cinema: the same people were going, but less frequently. If yours was one of the dozen or so pictures a year that captured the international imagination you could make a substantial killing, but only one film in eight made a profit.

Above: *Bruce Lee, superstar of the Hong Kong-based kung-fu movies (nicknamed "chop socky" by Variety) starred in Hollywood's first venture into the genre,* **Enter the Dragon** *(1973), in which a martial arts master helps British Intelligence corner opium smugglers. Lee died in 1973, the year of the film's release.*

Far right: *Most grueling of the "buddy" movies was* **Papillon** *(1973), the unrelenting film that Franklin J. Schaffner made from Henri Charrière's account of life in and escape from the penal colony on Devil's Island. Steve McQueen was the French safecracker imprisoned there; Dustin Hoffman played the fellow-convict with whom he forms a bond.*

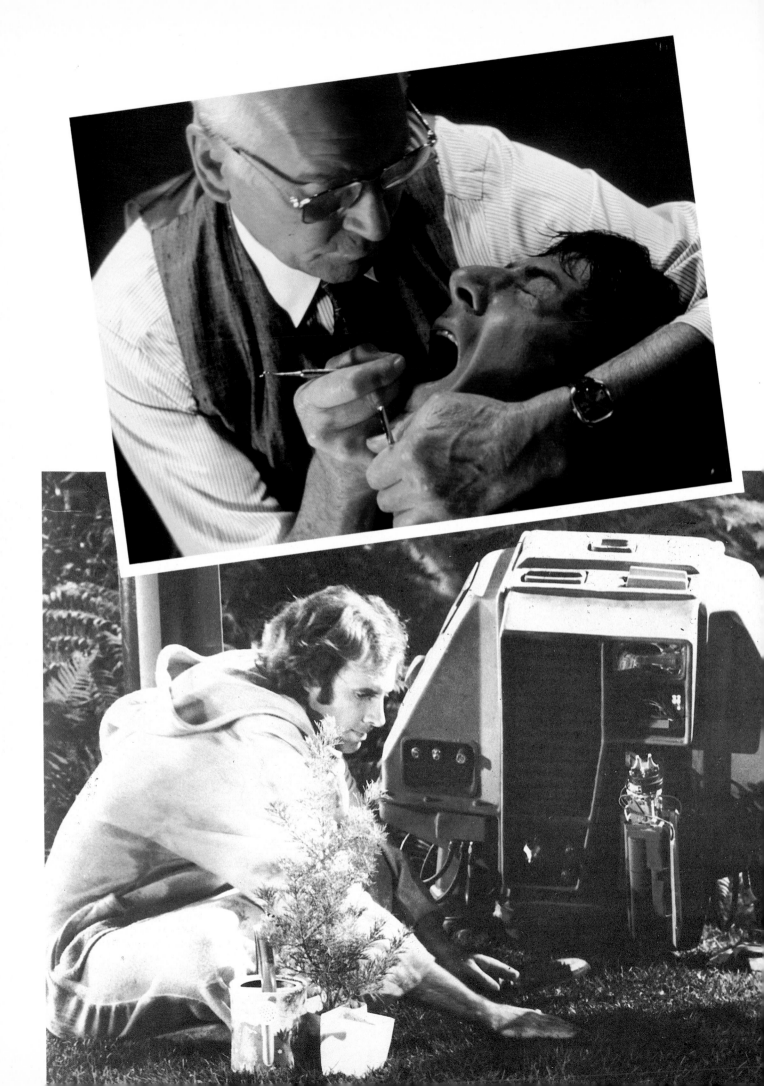

Left: *Dustin Hoffman starred in John Schlesinger's taut thriller* **Marathon Man** *(1976) as a Jewish student who stumbles into Nazis in modern New York. Laurence Olivier was memorable as their leader, a polite sadist whose way of extracting information is to tour his victim's mouth with a dentist's drill.*

Bottom left: *Douglas Trumbull's* **Silent Running** *(1972) was an unsung science fiction movie set aboard a huge space freighter on a long-term mission. The little droids prefigure R2-D2 and C-3PO of the* **Star Wars** *cycle. They are actually planting trees in this ecological tract, but they might as well be sowing the seeds for Spielberg's* **Close Encounters of the Third Kind** *(1977), for which movie Trumbull was later to design the effects. Bruce Dern was the lonely pioneer who preferred plants to people.*

Right: *Robert Redford and Jane Fonda were tellingly cast in Sydney Pollack's* **The Electric Horseman** *(1979), he as a former rodeo champion now reduced to advertising breakfast cereals, she as a reporter who follows his trail when he steals a champion horse and heads for the wide open spaces.*

The state-of-the-art special effects that marked Stanley Kubrick's **2001: A Space Odyssey** (1968) – along with those in Douglas Trumbull's comparatively unsung **Silent Running** (1972) – set the standards for the decade, while the "Star Wars" cycle and Spielberg's **Close Encounters of the Third Kind** (1977) brought into the live-action cinema the kind of magic for which audiences had hitherto looked to the Disney animators. It was the vogue for fantasy and science-fiction features that restored the studios themselves to favor, for the swing to location filming in the early Seventies had resulted not only in significant financial savings but in a fresh realism that audiences clearly found appealing.

Formula for success

As the risks and potential rewards for film-makers became greater, there was a marked reluctance to abandon successful formulas. Whereas series had always been popular with audiences – from "Lassie" to the Andy Hardy pictures – the sequel or continuation was now doubly attractive to the backers.

Not only could the same audience probably be induced back into the cinema once more, but there were also budgetary advantages. Alexander and Ilya Salkind, wizards of international financing who prospered in the Seventies, went to Spain to make **The Three Musketeers** (1973) and came back with enough footage to justify two features. Up to that point the choice would have seemed to have been between two options: edit the film right back and leave some of the most expensive scenes on the cutting-room floor, or release it in a three-hour-plus version that might have audiences wriggling in their seats and which would in any event dent the movie's earning power since fewer performances a day means less revenue. The Salkinds hit on a new solution. With only a few irate agents to face, they edited

Above: Nostalgia for the heyday of the Hollywood musical was catered to by an admirable compilation, **That's Entertainment** (1974), which included highlights from MGM movies from the previous half-century.

Top left: Sidney Lumet's **Network** (1976), a sharp-toothed satire of network television and the ratings war (Paddy Chayefsky wrote the screenplay) won Oscars both for Faye Dunaway as the power-hungry executive and for Peter Finch (who died before he could receive the award) as the paranoid presenter whose mental breakdown was presented nightly as segments of prime-time entertainment.

Bottom far left: Constance (Raquel Welch), a respectable bourgeois wife, is not entirely constant by nature and has to hide her Musketeer lover when the Cardinal's Men pay an early-morning call in **The Three Musketeers** (1974), Richard Lester's send-up of the Dumas novel and, so he claims, "the best Panamanian film ever made," since the production company was registered for convenience under the flag of Panama.

Below: Richard Attenborough's **A Bridge Too Far** (1977) was one of the very few World War II films to surface in the Seventies. Immaculately made and extravagantly cast, it was a no-expense-spared reconstruction of the events leading up to the tragic defeat of the airborne Allied troops at Arnhem in 1944.

their footage into two separate films, **The Three Musketeers** and **The Four Musketeers** (1975). The Salkinds followed their own example in shooting key scenes for **Superman II** (1981) while they had the cast and component parts assembled for **Superman the Movie** (although a legal-minded Brando ensured that his own out-takes never saw the light of day in the second installment).

The reluctance to abandon a winning formula was never more understandable than in the case of **Rocky** (1976). Sylvester Stallone had written the character (of a none-too-bright boxer who gets a crack at the world title) with himself in mind. Even though films with a sporting theme were supposedly anathema, he found several producers willing to gamble on the script, but none who would accept him in the role of the Philadelphia southpaw. Finally he got the ending his Cinderella story deserved when **Rocky** took the Best Film Oscar and vindicated his faith in the project. John G. Avildsen had

Left: *In the opening sequence of **Superman the Movie** (1978) the destruction of the planet Krypton forces Marlon Brando and Susannah York to send their son to Earth for safety....*

Right: *Clint Eastwood's first Western as director was the diabolic **High Plains Drifter** (1973) (later reworked in **Pale Rider** (1985)) in which he cast himself as a former lawman who comes back from the dead to take revenge on the townspeople who deserted him in his hour of need. It showed the influence of Sergio Leone, the Italian director of the Dollars Westerns, but nevertheless suggested that Eastwood's own visual style was a remarkable one.*

Bottom left: *In **Smokey and the Bandit** (1978), former stuntman Hal Needham directed his friend Burt Reynolds in a two-dimensional, cartoon-like chase. (Jackie Gleason was the incompetent lawman pursuing Reynolds' bootlegger.) A sequel followed, by which time Needham and Reynolds were pandering unashamedly to a redneck audience of good ole boys who just wanted to burn rubber and down beers.*

Above: *Rocky II* (1979) was the first of the films featuring the Philadelphia southpaw actually to be directed by Sylvester Stallone. The original's punchy realism was already giving way to the mythical glad-ragging that would keep the series a firm favorite for another decade.

Top right: *The last film of one of the true legends of the American cinema, John Wayne. Don Siegel's* **The Shootist** *(1976) cast him as an old gunslinger coming to roost in turn-of-the-century Nevada to die of cancer. Siegel was able to draw on earlier Wayne movies in order to build up the elegiac sense of myth; James Stewart, Lauren Bacall and Richard Boone (seen here) were also in this testamentary movie.*

Farewell to the OK Corral

been entrusted with the direction, but Stallone undertook that task as well in the inevitable (and comparably exciting) **Rocky II** (1979) made three years later. Parts III and IV of the story followed in the Eighties.

Other film-makers had less incentive to repeat themselves but, by the end of the Seventies, **Jaws**, **The Omen** (1976), **The Exorcist** (1973), **Death Wish** (1974) and **Superman** were just a few of the films that were to reappear with Roman numerals after their titles. At least the "Star Wars" cycle was conceived by George Lucas as a trilogy (and part of a larger plan), while Steven Spielberg, surprisingly, remains alone as a director who has returned to a popular film, **Close Encounters of the Third Kind**, and re-edited it to supply a "special edition" (1980). Although he is the first to do this, claiming that cinema should not be regarded as a dry-cement process, he will almost certainly not be the last.

Some of the genres and themes that emerged in the Seventies are discussed elsewhere in this book, but two stalwarts of the old Hollywood underwent radical revision. The Western, which might well have been popular with film-makers eager to make location pictures for just a fistful of dollars, went into a steep decline, suffering two unexpected blows when the immortal John Wayne is shot dead in **The Cowboys** (1972) and then plays an elderly gunslinger dying from cancer in **The Shootist** (1976) (the "Duke" himself succumbed to the same disease in 1979, just three years after his last film appearance in Don Siegel's moving homage). The revival of the Western by Michael Cimino in **Heaven's Gate** (1980), a picture doomed to commercial disaster and unfair critical calumny, did nothing to aid the genre's ailing fortunes. In any event, with the advent of the vigilante thriller and the tough city cop, the lawman's badge was pinned to the lapel of the urban cowboy. Clint Eastwood

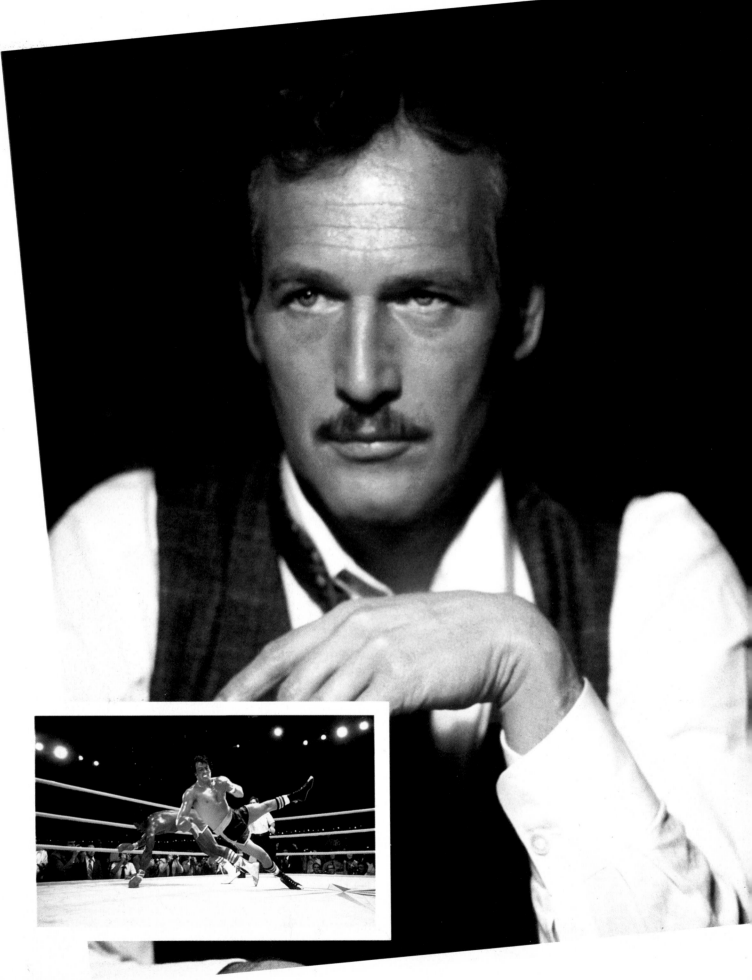

had exchanged his horse for a motorcycle as early as **Coogan's Bluff** (1968) while **Dirty Harry** (1971) gave him, after the poncho-clad Man with No Name from the Sergio Leone Westerns, the second of his great screen characters.

The war film also petered out, though the intelligent and intimate epic **Patton** (1970) drew audiences (and won a rejected Oscar for its star, George C. Scott). Later in the decade **Midway** (1976), a conventional World War II story, looked for success in Sensurround but without much luck or profit. The more recent war in Vietnam tended to be examined through the trauma of homecoming veterans (**Taxi Driver** (1976) and **The Deer Hunter** (1978) represented the

fiercer face of this drama) rather than through scenes of the conflict itself. It wasn't until the watershed of Francis Ford Coppola's **Apocalypse Now** (1979) that the scales tipped: the Reaganite bullishness of karate-chopping Chuck Norris and of Stallone's **First Blood** (1982) and **Rambo: First Blood Part II** (1985) still lay in the future.

For the purpose of easy analysis it is maddening that no discernible trend emerges from the list of box-office champions of the Seventies, yet for this we must be thankful since their variety argues the public's refusal to be pigeonholed. Were it otherwise, Hollywood would surely be as predictable as a factory conveyor belt. **Star Wars** (1977) was

Left: *Capitalizing on the phenomenally successful teaming of Paul Newman and Robert Redford in* **Butch Cassidy and the Sundance Kid** *(1969), George Roy Hill's confidence trickster comedy* **The Sting** *(1973) reunited the actors in a twisty Thirties tale of bluff and double-bluff. Marvin Hamlisch's arrangements immortalized the hitherto little-known piano rags of Scott Joplin. Newman plays Henry Gondorff, gambler and conman extraordinaire.*

Bottom left: *At the end of* **Rocky II** *(1979), Rocky (Sylvester Stallone) fights a rematch with Apollo Creed (Carl Weathers) and both men go down for the count — but Rocky is the first up, at 10.*

Right: *The three friends (Robert De Niro, Christopher Walken and John Savage) have escaped from Vietcong captivity, but their troubles are far from over in* **The Deer Hunter** *(1978).*

Below: *Francis Coppola's* **Apocalypse Now** *(1979) was a vast undertaking that nearly bankrupted this maverick director. Costs escalated; a leading actor (Martin Sheen) suffered a heart attack; typhoons wrecked one vast set. Coppola showed the movie to the Cannes Film Festival as a "work in progress" and admitted that he had had to mortgage his home to safeguard a final budget that was in excess of $30 million. Yet the film was its own vindication, drawing (uncredited) on Joseph Conrad's novella Heart of Darkness to provide an electrifying picture of the madness and monstrosity of the Vietnam war.*

the undisputed leader: otherwise there was one science-fiction film, a thriller, two musicals, a horror film, a crime thriller and two comedies. With the exceptions of **Grease** (1978), **The Sting** (1973) and **National Lampoon's Animal House** (1978), they are all intense pictures that would be diminished considerably by home viewing. Only three rely on stars for their appeal, **The Sting**, **Grease** and **Saturday Night Fever**, the last two leaning heavily on the talents of a contemporary phenomenon, John Travolta. **National Lampoon's Animal House** owes its popularity to the evergreen appeal of sophomore humor, while some would claim that the success of **The Godfather** (1972) was due in part to the reputation of Mario Puzo's book. Personally, I think the film developed its own "must-see" mystique, just as **The Exorcist** outgrew entirely the attractions of William Peter Blatty's novel.

Films were more attractively packaged, from the consumer's standpoint, and more aggressively marketed in the Seventies. Studio complacency and a system by which films earned automatic release had been banished and, in considering films as individual items for specialized treatment, target marketing was now becoming a reality. The increased showings of film on television and the boom in video recorders meant that the appetite for and awareness of movies was probably larger than at any previous point in the history of the cinema. Only the cinemas were letting the industry down. In the richer, leisure-oriented countries, prospective cinemagoers were moving away from the city centers which contained the old picture palaces. Only once or twice a year would audiences abandon the home screen to go to the cinema.

Above: *Sophomore humor was given its head of steam in John Landis's* **National Lampoon's Animal House** *(1978), set in 1962 and pitting Delta fraternity slobs against the Omega elite, as well as the hard-pressed faculty. Pretty girls decorate the scene – but the frat-house boys have most of the fun.*

Right: *In* **The Sting** *(1973), the aptly named conman Johnny Hooker (Robert Redford) shares his luck with his first partner (Robert Earl Jones), who is about to be killed by a big-time gangster. The rest of the picture turns on a revenge plot to even the score, though by extracting money instead of blood it hurts the bad guy more. Ironically Redford was Oscar-nominated for this role, though he missed out with his superior performance in* **Butch Cassidy and the Sundance Kid** *(1969).*

Law, Disorder & Other Fears

Chapter 2

Look into Hollywood's crystal ball for an adjective to describe this decade and only one leaps out: anxious. The anxiety was about the future of an industry pushed to the wall by the ever-present threat from television and the proliferation of home video systems, an industry caught in an inflationary spiral that had lost direction and lost confidence in the supremacy of its stars. The faceless boards of geographically distant banks and oil companies were giving approval to movie projects, uncomfortable replacements for the terrible tycoons of previous eras, larger-than-life characters who had been famous for their faults and philistinism but who had nevertheless lived "above the shop" and had movies in their blood.

There was anxiety about "the human condition," no longer confined to concern about growing up in the shadow of the Bomb (a movie generation had come to adulthood that had never known the absence of that threat) but now extended to a myriad of stress factors in everyday life, breakdowns not only of the individual but of local communities and of society itself. Political terrorism had hit previously unthinkable scales, while there was corruption in the highest of places and a war in Southeast Asia, whose aftermath seemed more traumatic to many Americans than had the actual distant conflict itself.

There was anxiety too about our own roles within a troubled society. The safe stereotypes in which the old Hollywood had traded were abandoned and a new realism took the movies by storm, giving a platform to political, social and sexual minorities. Where once the movies had been an escape, a panacea, they were now a confrontation, a mirror held up to our lives. The cinema may only record key events (such as America's disgraced President bidding a manic farewell to a betrayed electorate as helicopter blades flattened the lawns of the White House) in newsreels, but such facts and their significance form the very foundations of many of the films of the Seventies.

Cracks in the mirror

Art reflects life and, just as the cheerful, optimistic movies of the Thirties and Forties were planned to soothe worries about Depression and war, so the more edgy films of the Seventies addressed our more anxious condition.

Law and order — its imposition, its maintenance, its abuse — was central to the decade's movies. There had been an unprecedented decline in public morale in the wake of the Vietnam War and America had had to accept with muted disbelief the resignations of both its

Right: In **A Clockwork Orange** (1971), Malcolm McDowell was Alex, the lethal teenage thug, an aggressor turned into a victim by aversion therapy, losing his taste for rape, violence and murder to the singalong tune of "Singin' in the Rain".

President and its Vice-President. Then hitherto honored names like Kissinger and Rockefeller were accused over one matter or another. America was not alone: Britain was rocked by the Poulson affair and then further shocked by the attempted disappearance of one of its Members of Parliament, a former government minister. The Prime Minister of India was convicted of corrupt electoral practice and when her Opposition clamored noisily for her resignation, she promptly threw them into jail. The Chancellor of West Germany, the respected Willy Brandt, had to resign following a spy trial.

Hardly surprising, in the light of these events, that films about police and policing proliferated. Screen cops were often portrayed as corrupt, but that corruption was less often a premeditated abuse of their office than a delinquent demonstration of the dismay and disappointment in the morality of the force they had entered in good faith. **Serpico** (1974) and **Report to the Commissioner** (1975) were two remarkable true stories of widespread corruption set within the New York and Los Angeles Police Departments.

The Seventies also saw a marked increase in street violence. The fantasy world of **A Clockwork Orange** (1971), so brilliantly visualized by Stanley Kubrick and Anthony Burgess, was becoming more and more of a reality. Audiences were lapping up such violence,

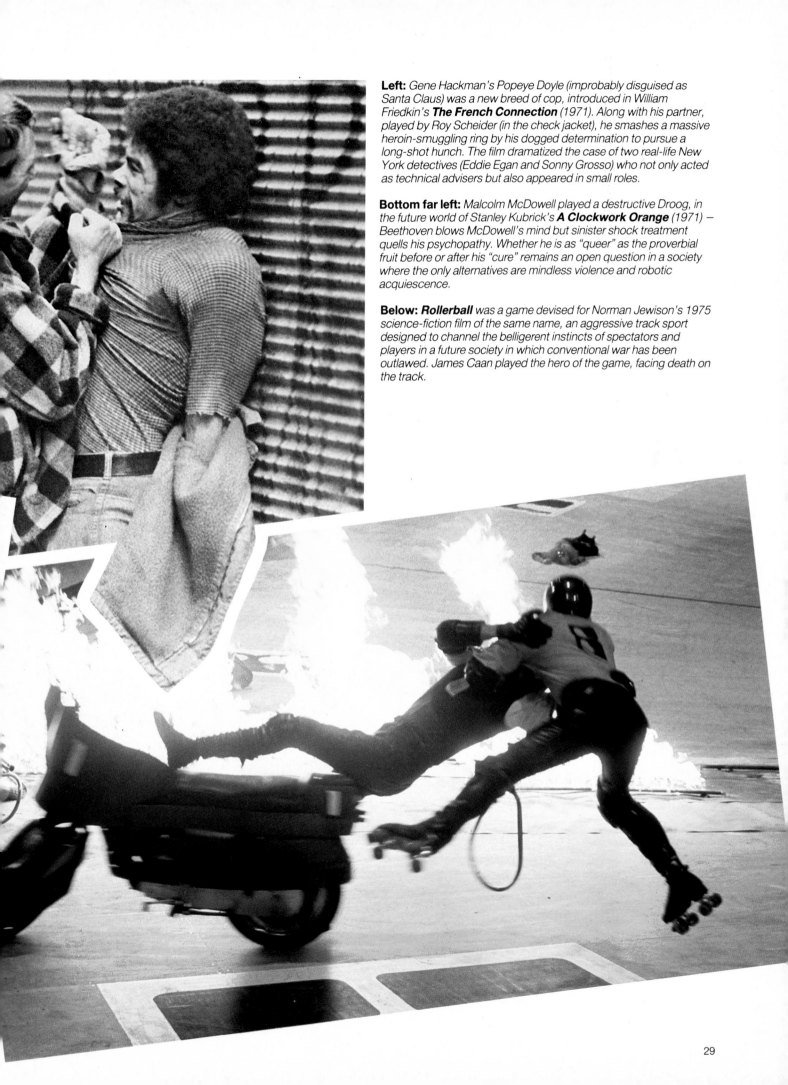

Left: *Gene Hackman's Popeye Doyle (improbably disguised as Santa Claus) was a new breed of cop, introduced in William Friedkin's **The French Connection** (1971). Along with his partner, played by Roy Scheider (in the check jacket), he smashes a massive heroin-smuggling ring by his dogged determination to pursue a long-shot hunch. The film dramatized the case of two real-life New York detectives (Eddie Egan and Sonny Grosso) who not only acted as technical advisers but also appeared in small roles.*

Bottom far left: *Malcolm McDowell played a destructive Droog, in the future world of Stanley Kubrick's **A Clockwork Orange** (1971) – Beethoven blows McDowell's mind but sinister shock treatment quells his psychopathy. Whether he is as "queer" as the proverbial fruit before or after his "cure" remains an open question in a society where the only alternatives are mindless violence and robotic acquiescence.*

Below: ***Rollerball** was a game devised for Norman Jewison's 1975 science-fiction film of the same name, an aggressive track sport designed to channel the belligerent instincts of spectators and players in a future society in which conventional war has been outlawed. James Caan played the hero of the game, facing death on the track.*

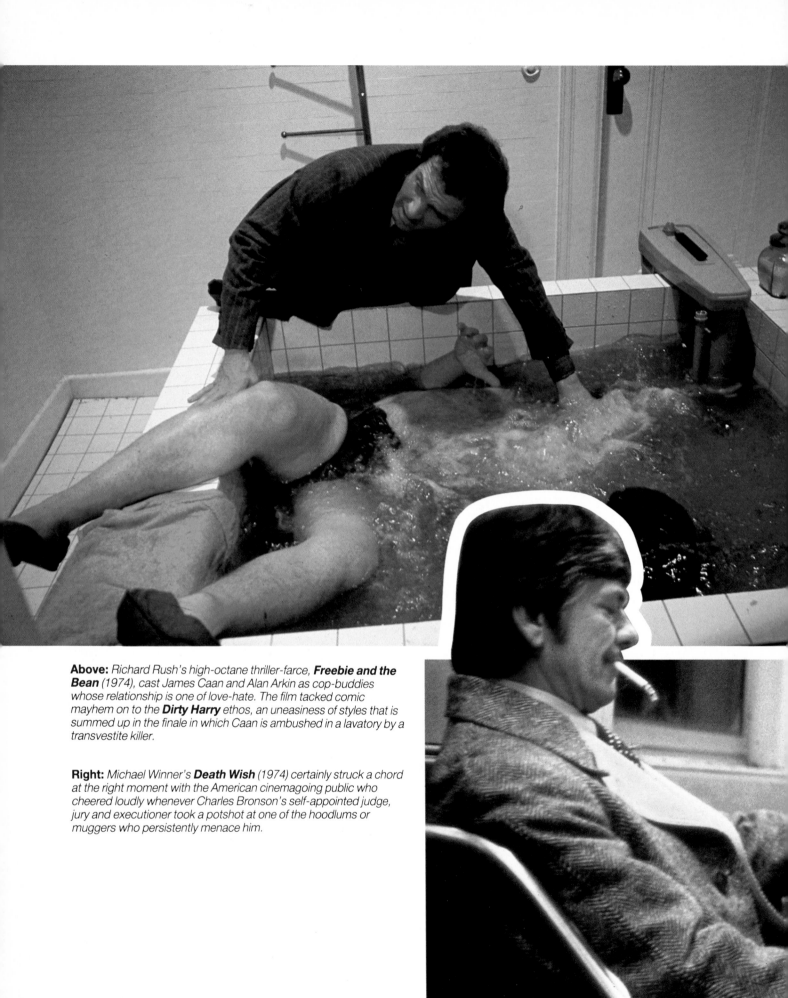

Above: Richard Rush's high-octane thriller-farce, **Freebie and the Bean** (1974), cast James Caan and Alan Arkin as cop-buddies whose relationship is one of love-hate. The film tacked comic mayhem on to the **Dirty Harry** ethos, an uneasiness of styles that is summed up in the finale in which Caan is ambushed in a lavatory by a transvestite killer.

Right: Michael Winner's **Death Wish** (1974) certainly struck a chord at the right moment with the American cinemagoing public who cheered loudly whenever Charles Bronson's self-appointed judge, jury and executioner took a potshot at one of the hoodlums or muggers who persistently menace him.

having been given a foretaste in Arthur Penn's **The Left-Handed Gun** (1958) and **Bonnie and Clyde** (1967) and Sam Peckinpah's **The Wild Bunch** (1969) and **Straw Dogs** (1971). What was new in the Seventies was the kung-fu movie, whose success was intimately bound up with Bruce Lee-style violence.

Movies like Robert Aldrich's **The Longest Yard** (1974) and Norman Jewison's **Rollerball** (1975) mirrored the violence in sport while, once police fallibility had been acknowledged, a sickening flood of law-and-order statements followed, most of which advocated private citizens' taking the law into their own hands. Clarence Darrow's statement that "the failure of justice itself may be more damaging to society than the crime" had never seemed truer. **Walking Tall** (1973), **Death Wish** and **Freebie and the Bean** (1974) were movies that put their tap roots down into the pool of anxiety over this issue. And there were, of course, the inimitable "Dirty Harry" movies. . . .

Cop . . . or criminal?

Clint Eastwood and director Don Siegel had already brought the Western to town in **Coogan's Bluff**, in which a rural lawman pursues his quarry into the confusing concrete jungle of the city. In **Dirty Harry** the pair looked dispassionately at city low-life and lawlessness. A cold, enigmatic and ruthless detective, Harry Callahan, sets out to capture a madman who strikes at random and demands a huge ransom if he is not to kill again. Callahan corners the killer but, after torturing him during the arrest, sees him set free because of legal niceties. The killer goes on another rampage and Harry's last act is to shoot him dead and then cast his badge aside in disgust at the job and the conditions under which he is supposed to perform it.

Far left: *The climax of* **Dirty Harry** *(1971) — Inspector Harry Callahan (Clint Eastwood) is about to execute the psychotic killer Aquarius without benefit of judge or jury. His SFPD badge then follows the corpse of the late childslayer beneath the murky waters of the quarry lake, thrown down in a gesture reminiscent of Gary Cooper's at the end of* **High Noon** *(1952).*

Below: **Taxi Driver** *(1976) starred Robert De Niro as a Vietnam veteran sickened by the decay of society as witnessed through the windshield of his yellow cab. He embarks on a murderous one-man mission to clean up the streets and through a perverse kind of heroism finds a point of entry into "normal" society.*

Below: *Even at his daughter's wedding, Don Vito Corleone (Marlon Brando),* **The Godfather** *in the 1972 adaptation of Mario Puzo's epic novel, is willing to listen to requests for favors or to right wrongs — but only for those who show "respect", which he values more than money.*

Bottom: *Opening with a huge close-up of keys hammering a sheet of paper, a striking metaphor for assassination by typewriter,* **All the President's Men** *(1976) was an always intelligent and resourceful filming of the Watergate investigations of Woodward and Bernstein. Robert Redford (right) and Dustin Hoffman added star luster to the roles of the crusading reporters, but the success was really that of the director, Alan J. Pakula.*

Dirty Harry was variously hailed and hated as a right-wing hymn to law and order, and it certainly spelled out with unarguable clarity the fact that the police often have to live by the rules of a brutal society if they are successfully to control it. But **Magnum Force** (1973), the film's sequel, pitted Harry against a cell of vigilante cops (the then comparatively unknown David Soul among their number) who act as judge, jury and executioner in exasperation over the number of felons escaping punishment from the congested and toothless courts. Harry makes his own violent stand against these miscreants, but too late — the vigilante was well on the way to becoming the Seventies' new screen hero.

One real-life model was Sheriff Buford Pusser of McNairy County, Tennessee, whose life (and death) was celebrated in a trilogy of movies, the first of which was **Walking Tall**. When appointed to office, Pusser believed absolutely in the axiom "Talk softly and carry a big stick." The election platform of the former wrestler had been the efficiency with which he had coped with a contretemps in a local casino. Pusser had had a major win that so displeased the management that they sent in their hired men to beat up Pusser and reclaim his winnings. When he had recovered, he took a home-made club and smashed his way back into the casino. "I fractured everybody's arms," he said proudly. "They tried me for armed robbery and acquitted me." He was promptly given a badge and the tacit license to fight fire with fire. Society saw him as a fitting hero; so did Hollywood and put the burly Joe Don Baker into **Walking Tall**.

The real Pusser suffered fifteen plastic surgery operations, the shooting away of part of his jaw and 200 stitches in his face following an ambush by those opposed to his regime. He died in a car crash while preparing to play himself in the second of the films, **Part 2, Walking Tall** (1975). The part was subsequently played by the Swedish actor Bo Svenson, who was also seen as Robert Redford's costar in **The Great Waldo Pepper** (1975). What had once had some pretense to being civic-minded action of a violent nature went on to become a vendetta of fury when Pusser's wife was killed in an

Right: *James Caan played the violent, unpredictable Sonny Corleone, son of Brando's Mafia dynasty chieftain in* **The Godfather** *(1972), Francis Coppola's powerful epic saga of organized crime from the mid-Forties to the mid-Fifties. Here Sonny deals with his wife-beating brother-in-law (Gianni Russo), a traitor to the Family who will shortly draw him into a fatal trap.*

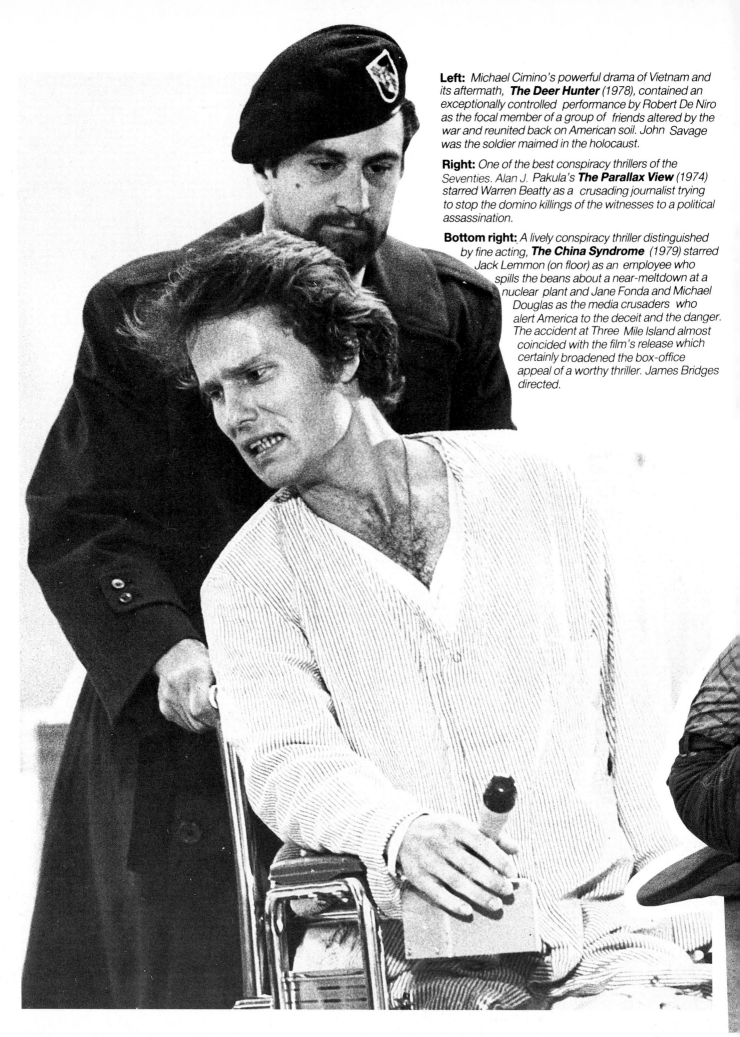

Left: *Michael Cimino's powerful drama of Vietnam and its aftermath, **The Deer Hunter** (1978), contained an exceptionally controlled performance by Robert De Niro as the focal member of a group of friends altered by the war and reunited back on American soil. John Savage was the soldier maimed in the holocaust.*

Right: *One of the best conspiracy thrillers of the Seventies. Alan J. Pakula's **The Parallax View** (1974) starred Warren Beatty as a crusading journalist trying to stop the domino killings of the witnesses to a political assassination.*

Bottom right: *A lively conspiracy thriller distinguished by fine acting, **The China Syndrome** (1979) starred Jack Lemmon (on floor) as an employee who spills the beans about a near-meltdown at a nuclear plant and Jane Fonda and Michael Douglas as the media crusaders who alert America to the deceit and the danger. The accident at Three Mile Island almost coincided with the film's release which certainly broadened the box-office appeal of a worthy thriller. James Bridges directed.*

ambush. "What's right is right, and you're the one that's gotta draw the line," is the encapsulation of the Pusser philosophy in the second film, an oversimplified statement that echoes the cliches of the traditional Westerns, "A man's gotta do what a man's gotta do" and "There are some things a man just can't walk around."

Despite the Pusser movies and such titles as **Gordon's War** (1973), **Vigilante Force** (1976) and **White Line Fever** (1975), the biggest international success of this group was Michael Winner's **Death Wish**, which had American audiences cheering in the cinemas as Charles Bronson takes his gun to snatch power from the impotent New York police, gunning down the muggers who hang around Central Park. He seeks revenge for his wife's murder and daughter's rape — yet when the police finally catch up with him they have to let him go since he has become a public hero. **Death Wish** inspired two sequels (both in the Eighties), by which time copycat vigilante violence had occurred on the New York subway.

Exterminating angel

The vigilante film reached its apotheosis with Martin Scorsese's excellent **Taxi Driver**. Robert De Niro's insomniac Vietnam veteran turns to taxi driving but is sickened and appalled by the seamy world that he sees through his windshield. Literally, a taxi driver is a man who will take anyone anywhere for money. No questions, no responsibility, no involvement; an embodiment of the spirit of urban alienation. But Scorsese is at pains to make his character mythic. He

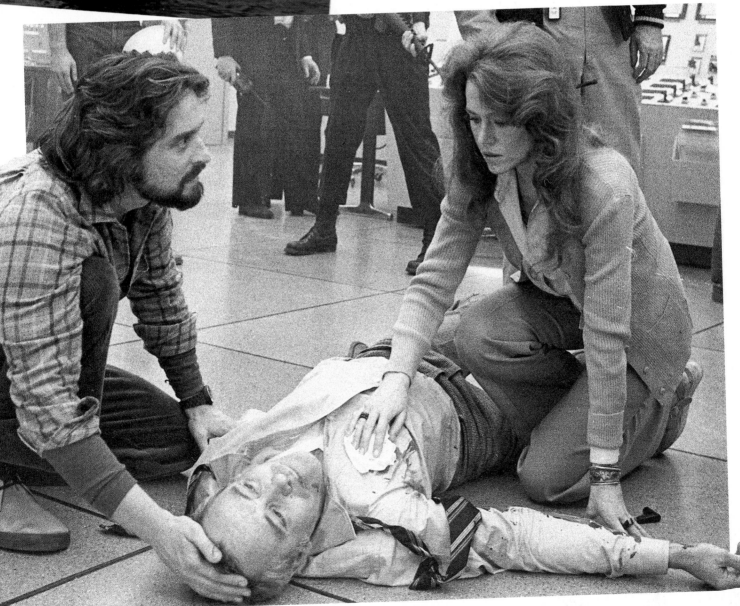

is an avenging angel, his cab a yellow chariot. He weighs the politicians and finds them wanting, he tries personal relationships and is rejected. Finally he retreats into his inner self, training and preparing for a conflict that is as apocalyptic as anything in the Book of Revelations.

De Niro kills and is himself seemingly killed, a bullet in his neck. But as the camera pans over the detritus of the mayhem, the walls as blood-spattered as those of an abattoir, Scorsese shifts gear and continues with a pan over a cleaner wall, this time decorated with newspaper cuttings acclaiming De Niro a hero for his night of massacre. The film ends with his rebirth when, for the first time, he establishes rapport with his fellow drivers, and ironically is able to feel coolly superior to the girl who spurned him. It is through the catharsis of operatic violence that a paranoid psychotic can finally achieve the status of hero.

The cinema of the Seventies was keen to debase the notion that the vigilante is someone who protects his own or society's interests in an imperfectly organized world. Active violence and bloodshed has a stronger box-office appeal than the chivalrous conduct of a sidewalk Superman. Yet the most notable vigilante action of this century was

Below: *While clearly deriving from the much superior **Rosemary's Baby** (1968), **The Exorcist** (1973) itself spawned not only a sequel (1977) but a shortlived host of imitations. The demonic possession of a young girl, Regan (Linda Blair) – named after King Lear's most wicked daughter – surely reflects US anxieties about the family, the generation gap, youthful rebellion and, above all, drugs – which "possessed" so many in the long aftermath of the hippie period, not yet concluded. Since much youthful protest was over the Vietnam War – which destroyed or distorted so many young lives (not all of them Vietnamese) – perhaps parents thought their children were also "possessed" by Communist sympathies, while young people enjoyed the spectacle of parents and priests disturbed and frightened.*

Right and bottom right: *A stylish remake of the Don Siegel classic of the Fifties, Philip Kaufman's **Invasion of the Body Snatchers** (1978) set the takeover of humans by seed-pods from another planet in contemporary San Francisco and cast Donald Sutherland, Brooke Adams, Jeff Goldblum and Veronica Cartwright as the quartet fighting the extra-terrestrial menace.*

taken in the Seventies and has also been documented in a movie. It was called **All the President's Men** (1976).

The uncovering of the Watergate conspiracy and the subsequent protracted end of the Nixon era in America was like the lancing of a boil. America likes little better than to seek in the movies a metaphor for the state of the nation, whether in sprawling epics like **The Godfather** and **The Deer Hunter** or smaller chronicles such as **Easy Rider** and John Milius' **Big Wednesday** (1978). The movies about Vietnam and the trauma of coming home to a disinterested and ungrateful civilian population gradually yielded to other studies of urban paranoia. Themes of conspiracy were common – in the Kennedy assassination hypothesis, **Executive Action** (1973); in Alan J. Pakula's **The Parallax View** (1974) and in Larry Cohen's **The Private Files of J. Edgar Hoover** (1978); in Peter Hyams' space confidence-trick, **Capricorn One** (1978); in the chilling medical conspiracy, **Coma** (1978); in the alarming cover-up of a nuclear near-disaster, **The China Syndrome** (1979). But it was **All the President's Men**, the Robert Redford-produced film of the book by investigative journalists Bob Woodward (Redford) and Carl Bernstein (Dustin Hoffman), that aired most specifically, directly and thoroughly the Watergate closet.

The basic paranoia of the times is amusingly caught in a line from the comedy **Semi-Tough** (1977), directed by Michael Ritchie. An anxious young man is pressed into service as an usher at a wedding. He protests that he doesn't know what is required of him. It is patiently explained that all he has to do is seat the bride's relations on one side of the aisle and the groom's on the other. "But how do I know which is which?" he inquires. "You *ask* them!" cries his irritated mentor. Sad to let go of his imaginary worry-beads, the prospective usher continues, "But suppose they lie. . . ."

The supposition and fear that people were lying to us clangs echoingly around many of these films. A new version of **Invasion of the Body Snatchers** (1978), with Donald Sutherland in danger of being taken over by an alien lifeform, supplies an offbeat expression of that contemporary angst and the fears of conspiracy. Significantly, the same science-fiction story had already served as a political allegory as long ago as 1956, when Don Siegel directed and McCarthy's anti-Communist hysteria, not Watergate, was the name of the game.

Top right: *William Friedkin's **The Exorcist** (1973) was a superior horror movie with the power and spectacular special effects to induce nightmares. Linda Blair played the little girl possessed by a demon, Ellen Burstyn her mother and Max von Sydow the elderly exorcist on the case. But it is another priest (Jason Miller) who finally expels the demon, at the cost of his life.*

Right: *Unaware that well-intentioned crib-swapping took place shortly after she gave birth, Lee Remick mothers the anti-Christ in **The Omen** (1976). Damien, the little devil with a birthmark in the shape of a configuration of sixes on his scalp, survived to appear in the two sequels; for Miss Remick, motherly love went unrewarded ....*

Far right: *Patrick Troughton, paddling in the shallow waters of Satanism, is skewered by a falling lightning conductor turning him into a priestly kebab. **The Omen**, classiest of a whole school of devil-may-care horror movies, was stylishly directed by Richard Donner.*

Later on, as social worries became less specific, the cinema addressed them as it always has, with a stronger shift towards the thriller and horror genres, with shockers like **The Exorcist**, **Jaws**, **The Omen** and **Alien** (1979), all of which gave rise to sequels. A parallel phenomenon was the cycle of disaster movies that enjoyed a brief vogue in the Seventies. These again spoke calmingly to our nervous fears by making us live vicariously through unimaginable terrors.

Fun with phobias

Ronald Neame's **The Poseidon Adventure** (1972) was the first major success, putting a weird conglomeration of humanity at peril in an ocean liner turned upside down by a freak wave. The series gathered momentum in 1974 in which year alone the deliciously cross-eyed Karen Black piloted a crippled 747 jet-liner in the

Above: *Things are looking dicey on board the 747: a private plane has just crashed through the cockpit, an assortment of gibbering humanity is fretting in cabin class, the crew are dead or unconscious and there is only a stewardess to fly the plane. Worse still, it is Karen Black who is cross-eyed.* **Airport 1975** *(1974) took the disaster movie to fresh heights of absurdity but its tongue was in its cheek.*

Left: *An early warning of the disaster movie cycle came in* **The Poseidon Adventure** *(1972), in which a freak wave turns over an ocean liner transporting the usual Hollywood grab-bag of assorted characters. Priest-with-doubts Gene Hackman wrestles with the weighty problem of delaying Shelley Winters' arrival in the next world. Veteran British director Ronald Neame helped color the stereotypes with real fondness.*

Above: *Best and most ambitious of the group jeopardy thrillers was* **The Towering Inferno** *(1974), in which a skyscraper goes ablaze during the inauguration ceremony and a host of VIPs are trapped on the 136th floor. Decent architect Paul Newman comes to the rescue (aided by Fire Chief Steve McQueen).*

Above: *Charlton Heston was one of the more mature actors who had to contend with the natural demolition of California in* **Earthquake** *(1974), the disaster movie that introduced Sensurround, an emission of low-frequency sound that gave the audience a headache almost as bad as the one inflicted by the script. British-born veteran matte artist Albert Whitlock, who worked on some of Hitchcock's later films, supervised the special effects photography, creating many of the backgrounds.*

prematurely-titled **Airport 1975** ("You mean the stewardess is flying the plane?" cried a terrified passenger, thereby laying the foundation of the satirical comedy film **Airplane!** (1980)); Charlton Heston and fellow stars fought against the complete annihilation of California by **Earthquake**; fireman Steve McQueen teamed up with architect Paul Newman to save trapped celebrities from **The Towering Inferno**, a huge 136-story skyscraper that goes ablaze during the inauguration ceremony. And in the same year as this woe-laden trio, the British cinema also weighed in with Richard Lester's **Juggernaut**, about a terrorist bomb planted aboard a storm-lashed cruise liner.

However robust the beginnings of this cycle, it was to fizzle out ingloriously with half-baked spectacles such as **Avalanche** (1978) and the decline of producer Irwin Allen in **The Swarm** (1978) (killer bees destroying Houston), **Beyond the Poseidon Adventure** (1979) (a mistaken return to the watery scene of former glories) and the papier-maché volcano drama, **When Time Ran Out** (1980).

The disaster movie and the conspiracy thriller are joined by Steven Spielberg's monster hit, **Jaws**, which built Peter Benchley's best-selling novel about a marauding killer shark and the reactions of the townspeople whose tourist beaches the hungry beast is depopulating, into a masterpiece of terror-suspense. This hugely successful film not only opened the trilogy of watery Benchley thrillers to be filmed − **The Deep** (1977) and **The Island** (1980) were the two that followed − but rewarded Hollywood's faith in the young Steven Spielberg, who had previously made only one feature, **The Sugarland Express** (1974): all his earlier work had been television films, including **Duel** (1971), in which he had turned a story of a motorist being menaced by a giant truck into a similarly abstract exercise in terror.

Far left: *Second of a watery trilogy of films deriving from the novels of Peter Benchley -* **Jaws** *(1975) came before it,* **The Island** *(1980) after.* **The Deep** *(1977) starred Jacqueline Bisset and Nick Nolte as treasure-seekers who became entangled in voodoo and drug-smuggling off the coast of Bermuda. Peter Yates directed with misplaced conviction.*

Left: *The world's tallest building lights up the San Francisco sky in* **The Towering Inferno** *(1974) − giving the contract (for electrical wiring) to the lowest bidder does not always pay, as architect Richard Chamberlain discovers at the cost of his life.*

A Funny Sense of Humor

Chapter 3

Comedy came out of the closet in the Seventies, out of the family den and into a less constrained and more adult area. Carefully assembled comedy packages were replaced by the highly personal output of a number of former television gagsmiths – Carl Reiner, Mel Brooks and Woody Allen among them – who had labored for Sid Caesar on television's legendary *Your Show of Shows*.

Their work swept away the svelte bedroom comedies that had kept Rock Hudson, Doris Day and Cary Grant in almost constant employment during the first half of the previous decade. Nothing risqué was ever allowed to erupt through the mirrored calm of those Universal fantasies. That would have been as unthinkable as Doris Day going to bed in curlers or waking up without a fresh coat of lipstick. It was simply impossible for audiences any longer to accept the rigid sexual propriety of these impossibly well-bred and well-behaved characters.

America was heading for social, sexual and moral precipices. Landmarks along that route were pointed out by iconoclastic but isolated movies such as **Bob & Carol & Ted & Alice** (1969) (psychological), **M∗A∗S∗H** (1970) (sociological) and the later **Shampoo** (1975) (sexual and political). In the face of this ruthless advance, former box-office comedy champions like Bob Hope and Jerry Lewis retired gracefully. The "family" comedy remained in the phenomenally successful domain of the disaster-prone Inspector Clouseau, a character created by Peter Sellers in the Blake Edwards film **The Pink Panther** in 1963. The role had been planned for Peter Ustinov, but Sellers took over as a last-minute replacement, growing a Victorian moustache as a sign of self-asserted masculinity that gave him the key to the bumbling Sûreté detective. The series, which continued until (and by some tasteless use of out-takes even after) Sellers' death, became the James Bond of comedy, a sequence of ever brasher and ever more expensive productions that became mechanical with time, although the Seventies saw huge box-office receipts for **The Return of the Pink Panther** (1974), **The Pink Panther Strikes Again** (1976) and **The Revenge of the Pink Panther** (1978).

Even though he rarely stretched his comic genius in his later years, Sellers was a uniquely gifted actor and mimic in the manner of his idol, Sir Alec Guinness, and a box-office champion whose endorsement could and did help a film like Mel Brooks' **The Producers** (1968) get off the ground. He called it "the ultimate film . . . the essence of all great comedy combined in a single picture . . . tragedy-comedy, comedy-tragedy, pity, fear, hysteria and a largesse

Right: *In the Neil Simon parody of* **Casablanca** *(1943) and* **The Maltese Falcon** *(1941),* **The Cheap Detective** *(1978), private-eye Lou (Peter Falk) interviews crippled millionaire Ezra Dezire (Sid Caesar) and his voluptuous wife Jezebel (Ann-Margret).*

MASH·142·91

of lunacy woven together with sheer magic. Those of us who have seen this film and understood it have experienced a phenomenon that occurs only once in a life span." It took audiences longer to respond to the unaccustomed savagery of Brooks' first film, but it did grow in reputation until by the end of the Seventies it had achieved the status of a cult comedy classic.

That film was a breakthrough, the point at which America began to allow iconoclastic humor to take center stage while the unarguably popular middle-class domestic comedies were left mumbling in the wings. King of the group thus demoted (except at the box-office) was Neil Simon, a gifted playwright with a seemingly endless supply of witty one-liners which he peppered through such homely comedies as **Barefoot in the Park** (1967), **The Prisoner of Second Avenue** (1975), **The Out-of-Towners** (1970) and **The Goodbye Girl** (1977).

Far left: *Robert Altman's sanguine black comedy* **M*A*S*H** *(1970) was a genuine shocker at the time of release, not only for its bloody depiction of life in the emergency operating wards of a Mobile Army Surgical Hospital, but also for its cheerful irreverence and unequivocal anti-war stance. Elliott Gould and Donald Sutherland were memorably teamed and Altman's freewheeling direction gave the feeling that the film was perilously balanced on a high wire above deep and dangerous waters. Here Trapper John (Gould) anesthetizes a colonel (J.B. Douglas).*

Top left: *By the time of* **Nickelodeon** *(1976) (with Ryan O'Neal and his daughter Tatum), the critics of the day were set to lacerate director Peter Bogdanovich. This gentle, leisurely comedy about the birth of the movies had a transparent love for its subject and bags of style.*

Below: *Former critic Peter Bogdanovich made a considerable impact as a director with the low-budget* **Targets** *(1968) and then* **The Last Picture Show** *(1971). Comparisons with the young Orson Welles proved unfortunate, for his talent was soon reviled and sometimes squandered.* **What's Up, Doc?** *(1972) was a deliciously tilted snoot at his movie mentors, a loving tribute to the screwball comedies of Hollywood's heyday, richly funny as Ryan O'Neal and Barbra Streisand untangle a skein of confusion involving identical tartan suitcases, and are chased all over San Francisco.*

Although he never appears in his own material, Simon was being marketed as a mainstream Woody Allen with happier endings and the angst control turned right down. He also shared with Allen a parodic liking of old movies, as was demonstrated in Simon's **Murder by Death** (1976), a glorious spoof of every detective movie ever made, and **The Cheap Detective** (1978), which, like Allen's **Play It Again, Sam** (1972), contained a humorous imitation of the classic romance **Casablanca** (1943).

The art of laughter

But *the* comic figure of the Seventies was unarguably writer-director-performer Woody Allen. He seemed the perfect bespectacled embodiment of our lives and anxious times. In his cabaret days he was once described as "a flat-headed, red-haired lemur with closely

Above: Neil Simon's **The Sunshine Boys** (1975) was a fond but abrasive comedy about two retired vaudevillians forced to revive their act for a television program. Old wounds are reopened, the flames of ancient enmity fanned: George Burns and Walter Matthau were magnificently grouchy as the feuding geriatrics.

Top left: Warren Beatty produced and starred in **Shampoo** (1975), a satirical farce set on the day of the election that brought Richard Nixon and Spiro Agnew to office. Beatty played a Beverly Hills hair stylist trying to keep his balance on the sexual merry-go-round and raise the finance to open his own salon. Julie Christie (on the receiving end of the dryer) and Goldie Hawn played girlfriends old and new. The director was Hal Ashby.

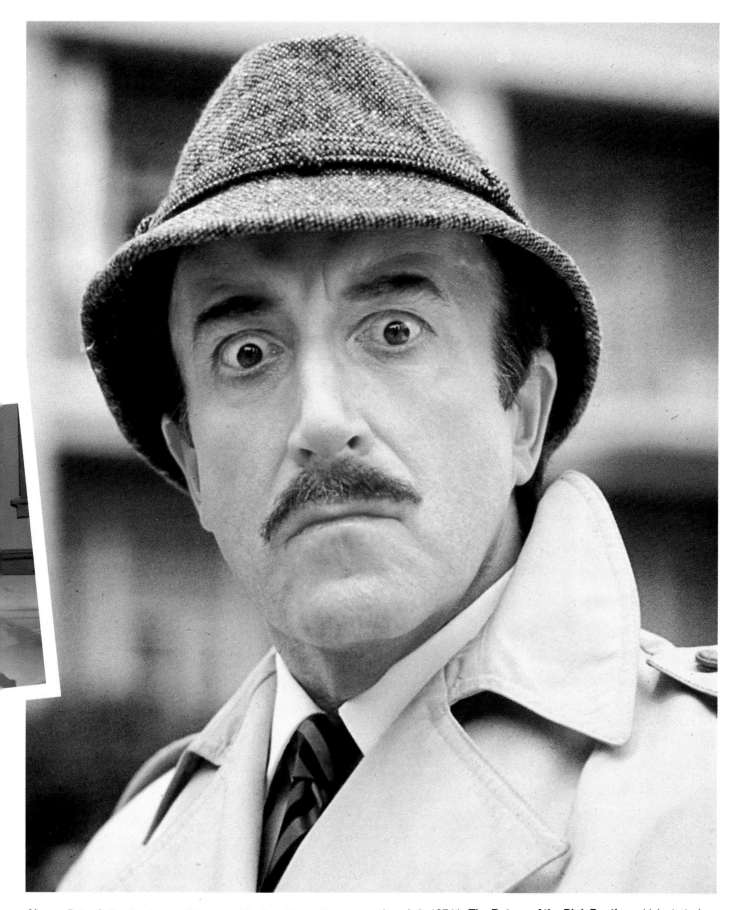

Above: Peter Sellers had created the role of the bumbling, Jacques Tati-inspired Inspector Clouseau in the 1963 comedy **The Pink Panther** and its sequel **A Shot in the Dark** (1964). Alan Arkin took the character over in **Inspector Clouseau** (1968). Sellers returned to the role in 1974 in **The Return of the Pink Panther** which started a series of phenomenally successful Seventies sequels, all directed by Blake Edwards. Using old footage and out-takes, the movies even survived Sellers' death in 1980.

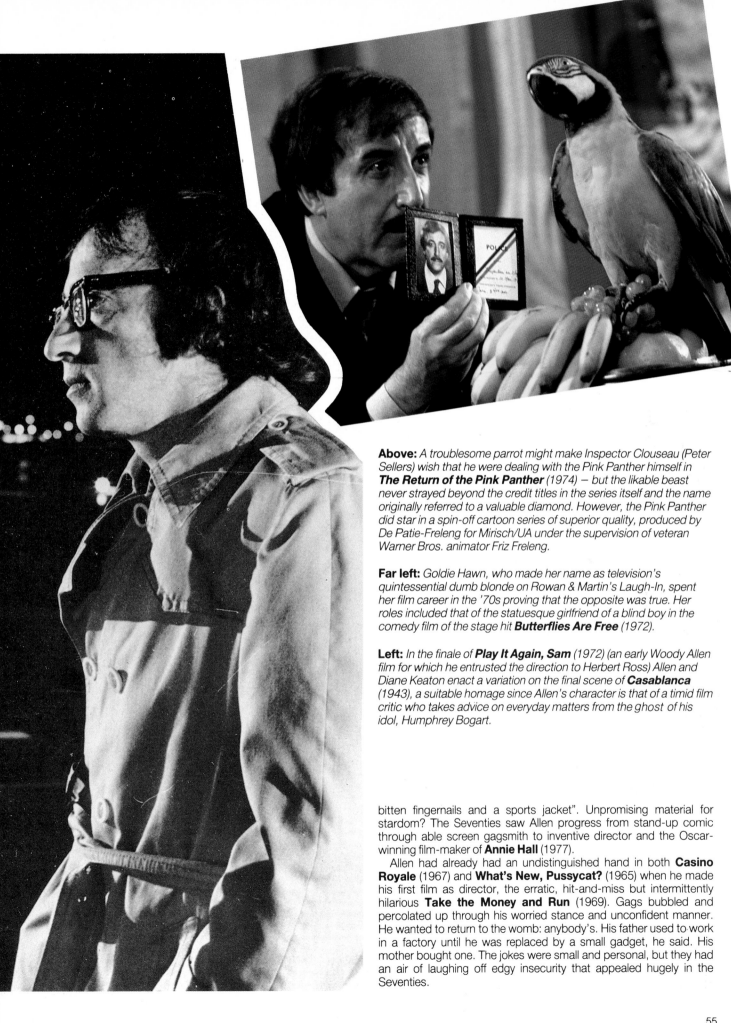

Above: *A troublesome parrot might make Inspector Clouseau (Peter Sellers) wish that he were dealing with the Pink Panther himself in* **The Return of the Pink Panther** *(1974) — but the likable beast never strayed beyond the credit titles in the series itself and the name originally referred to a valuable diamond. However, the Pink Panther did star in a spin-off cartoon series of superior quality, produced by De Patie-Freleng for Mirisch/UA under the supervision of veteran Warner Bros. animator Friz Freleng.*

Far left: *Goldie Hawn, who made her name as television's quintessential dumb blonde on Rowan & Martin's Laugh-In, spent her film career in the '70s proving that the opposite was true. Her roles included that of the statuesque girlfriend of a blind boy in the comedy film of the stage hit* **Butterflies Are Free** *(1972).*

Left: *In the finale of* **Play It Again, Sam** *(1972) (an early Woody Allen film for which he entrusted the direction to Herbert Ross) Allen and Diane Keaton enact a variation on the final scene of* **Casablanca** *(1943), a suitable homage since Allen's character is that of a timid film critic who takes advice on everyday matters from the ghost of his idol, Humphrey Bogart.*

bitten fingernails and a sports jacket". Unpromising material for stardom? The Seventies saw Allen progress from stand-up comic through able screen gagsmith to inventive director and the Oscar-winning film-maker of **Annie Hall** (1977).

Allen had already had an undistinguished hand in both **Casino Royale** (1967) and **What's New, Pussycat?** (1965) when he made his first film as director, the erratic, hit-and-miss but intermittently hilarious **Take the Money and Run** (1969). Gags bubbled and percolated up through his worried stance and unconfident manner. He wanted to return to the womb: anybody's. His father used to work in a factory until he was replaced by a small gadget, he said. His mother bought one. The jokes were small and personal, but they had an air of laughing off edgy insecurity that appealed hugely in the Seventies.

In his delightfully spare yet fanciful futuristic comedy **Sleeper** *(1973),* *Woody Allen plays a health-food store owner who is placed on ice* *and awakened 200 years hence to find a world gone farcically awry.* *To avoid capture (bottom far right) in this Brave New World of pills* *and orgasm machines (can it be Hollywood?), he has to pose as a* *robot slave when Diane Keaton gives a dinner party. But he revives* *the forgotten idea of Love and wins over Keaton, even when his* *wooing at a farm full of monstrous vegetables and animals* **(below)** *is* *subject to interruption.*

Allen's screen work has always been studded with references to other film-makers, his particular role model being the Swedish director Ingmar Bergman. But it was a humorous obsession with Humphrey Bogart that marked Allen's popular play, **Play It Again, Sam**, in which a timid and sexually gauche film critic is advised on matters of seduction by the ghost of his screen idol. ("Something wrong with sweat?" this apparition asks when Allen favors an alluring after-shave.) The film, in which Allen himself played the luckless Felix ("My wife called me a pervert because I drank our water-bed"), was directed by Herbert Ross and was the better disciplined for having a steady hand on the tiller. Allen's own directorial style in **Take the Money and Run** and **Bananas** (1971) (a comedy about revolution in a Latin-American dictatorship) was, to say the least, haywire. His idiosyncratic approach to writing and directing didn't start to win broad favor with the paying public until **Everything You Always Wanted to Know About Sex, But Were Afraid to Ask** (1972), a literal rendering of the sex manual that "contains every idea I have ever had about sex, including a few that led to my divorce!" Here he introduced us to a frustrated and overactive couple, a wary transvestite, a psychiatrist with a hopeless crush on a sheep and, in the hilarious finale sequence set inside the human body during intercourse, Allen himself as the parachutist sperm who doesn't want to come or go.

In his next film, **Sleeper** (1973), the hero wakes from hypersleep 200 years hence, worrying about the arrears of his Social Security payments while facing a bizarre new world in which sex remains his greatest problem. The subsequent **Love and Death** (1975) was set in the Russia of 1812 with Woody as a man condemned to death and reviewing the slapstick folly of his life in a pleasing parody of Tolstoy's *War and Peace*. These were art movies, unusual since they were comedies at a time when the art circuit rarely rocked with laughter; nor could Allen even be described as a box-office star. A straight acting role in Martin Ritt's passionate film **The Front** (1976), a study of the effects of McCarthy's anti-Communist hysterics on the witch-hunted television writers, did nothing to boost his broad appeal. It wasn't until the sublime **Annie Hall** took the Best Film, Director and Actress Oscars (Woody preferred to play jazz with his cronies in New York rather than fly out to the Californian society he satirized in the film) that there was a real shift of gears in his career and that of Diane Keaton, the starring actress on whom the character of Annie was loosely based. He followed that with **Interiors** (1978), a determinedly straight-faced study of a disturbed and self-destructive

Bottom left: *Neil Simon exercised his dry wit in a 1978 portmanteau comedy,* **California Suite** *(a companion piece to his 1971 Manhattan-based* **Plaza Suite***) and this time came up with four separate stories linked by the Los Angeles hotel in which the characters are staying. The final episode involved the trouble-plagued holiday of two black couples, the husbands played by Bill Cosby and Richard Pryor.*

Below: *One of the most spectacular of Woody Allen's comedies and one of the most consistently funny was* **Love and Death** *(1975), set in the Russia of the Napoleonic wars and casting the bespectacled comic as an anachronistically neurotic and anxious condemned man reviewing his life after an assassination attempt (unsuccessful, of course, since he kills a lookalike) on Napoleon himself. Since his chilly wife and cousin Sonia (played by Diane Keaton) habitually served meals made of snow and consistently avoided sex – at least, with him – perhaps execution could be considered something of a relief.*

Right: *Ryan O'Neal makes an ingenious quick getaway in* **Nickelodeon** *(1976). Peter Bogdanovich's comedy about the early days of moviemaking paid affectionate tribute to the Golden Age of silent comedy; this scene is reminiscent of Buster Keaton's classic short* **Neighbors** *(1920).*

Bottom right: *Significantly posed against a poster for a movie by his role-model Ingmar Bergman, Woody Allen and Diane Keaton were soon to win 1977 Oscars (he as Best Director, she as Best Actress) for* **Annie Hall**, *a sweet-and-sour examination of a relationship not unlike their own.*

Far right: *In the office comedy* **Nine to Five** *(1980), a tyrannical boss (Dabney Coleman) gets his comeuppance from a trio of formidable women. Blond country singer Dolly Parton made a debut as one of them (the other two were Jane Fonda and Lily Tomlin). She was also Oscar-nominated for the theme song, which she wrote and performed. The film sparked off a TV series in which three different actresses took the roles — but executive producer Jane Fonda made an occasional guest appearance.*

family that severely disappointed many of his newly acquired fans. **Manhattan** (1979) arguably became his best single film to date, magically bringing together the maypole strands of his talent.

Neuroses in New York

Less candidly autobiographical than **Annie Hall**, **Manhattan** mirrored honestly the joys, sorrows and dangers of being a 42-year-old New Yorker. Allen plays a writer of fatuous television sitcoms who impulsively quits his job to attempt to write a novel based on characters from among his coterie of modish Manhattanites. Right up to and including **Annie Hall**, Allen had used his witty one-liners as crutches to support what was still fundamentally the act of a stand-up comic. His need to raise a laugh and be loved may have been abandoned during the glum posturings of **Interiors**, but **Manhattan** drained off much of the cuteness from his act and gave it the hard edge of truth. The jokes were no longer jumping out seeking approval; they now rose organically from the characters and lay rooted in their haphazard, chaotic lives.

This was the promised comic masterpiece, the sweeter for the time it had been in coming. It was indeed everything we always wanted to know that Woody Allen could do but were afraid to ask of him.

If Allen's was the one comic talent that came to perfect fruition in the Seventies, there were others that cropped heavily. Carl Reiner started the decade by offering the monstrous black comedy **Where's Poppa?** (1970), which had an almost demonic energy in the way it drew up the battle lines between George Segal and his impossible Jewish mother, played to the hilt by Ruth Gordon. This fine actress, then well into her seventies, also played opposite the whey-faced young Bud Cort in the comparably dark **Harold and Maude** (1971). Reiner went on to incur the uncomfortable displeasure of the religious lobby by casting George Burns as the Almighty in

the lightweight and wholly inoffensive **Oh, God!** (1977) (For real offense, the religious Establishment had to wait for **Monty Python's Life of Brian** (1979).) Reiner also surfaced as the cinematic mentor of the explosively funny Steve Martin, though their one Seventies project, **The Jerk** (1979), was not up to the standard of the later **Dead Men Don't Wear Plaid** (1982), **The Man With Two Brains** (1983) or **All of Me** (1984).

Outbursts and rages

Gene Wilder emerged as a singular and special talent in **The Producers**. A graduate of the Actors Studio, Wilder had scored strongly in his first screen appearance, a striking cameo of a nervous young mortician abducted for a joyride fraught with danger by the outlaw heroes in **Bonnie and Clyde**. Mel Brooks' blazing bad-taste farce helped define Wilder's on-screen comic personality, for he has always excelled at playing characters who are nervous, anxious, jittery or paranoid. His specialty is the slow burn of worry followed by the catharsis of hysterical outbursts and towering rages. He adapted this pattern of behavior from his own childhood in which he had been forced to be quiet in the presence of his ailing mother: every so often the pent-up emotions would volcano forth, only to be followed by reconciliation and another long period of silent suffering.

In **The Producers** these qualities were invested in the character of an unprepossessing accountant who joins forces with an impresario (Zero Mostel) in seeking out the worst play that could possibly be produced on Broadway. By oversubscribing the production many times over but guaranteeing a closure on opening night, they plan to net a fortune by pocketing the overinvestment. They discover a pro-Nazi musical *Springtime for Hitler* (which was once to have been the film's title, though the distributor's caution prevailed) and watch in horror while the frozen stares of disbelief on opening night turn to wild applause when the audience hails the play as a comic masterpiece.

The Producers itself met with a similar stunned silence, but the disbelief lasted a little longer. Until, in fact, Peter Sellers' generous testimonial; after that, audiences tested the icy water of Brooks' savage comedy with wary toes. If the sick joke had already been accepted as guiltily cathartic, Brooks certainly took it to fresh extremes. Taboos were his instinctive targets and he tap-danced through the minefield of public opinion, the huge seeming folly of his approach winning him grudging admiration in some quarters. His next film was altogether cooler in temperature and safer in subject matter, an uneven farce set in pre-Revolutionary Russia, **The Twelve Chairs** (1970). Brooks himself played a small role in this story about three men seeking a fortune that has been stuffed into one of a dozen dining chairs.

Main picture: *In the outrageous black comedy* **Where's Poppa?** *(1970) love of girlfriend Trish Van Devere (right) leads George Segal to weigh up methods of disposing of his tiresome and eccentric mother Ruth Gordon (center). Carl Reiner's zany comedy became a cult success.*

Inset: *Reluctantly glamorized Glenda Jackson won her second Oscar in three years for* **A Touch of Class** *(1973), a spry adult comedy that touched a nerve with the public. George Segal plays the married American businessman who blunders into an affair with an astringent dress designer; Mel Frank wrote and directed it with a surface polish that distracted from the lack of originality in the material.*

Joking with genre

Brooks' next four films were parodies of specific film genres that went beyond the delight of buffs and *aficionados* to score more strongly with the public than did the films of his *Your Show of Shows* cowriter, Woody Allen. Broader meant better at the box-office and **Blazing Saddles** (1973) was a literally flatulent explosion of the clichés of the Western film, attacked by one American critic for a plot that sagged like a tenement washing line. But Brooks' very style was more and more to create a revue-style parody and pack it haphazardly with gags, rather like cramming students into a telephone box. Narrative never is and never was his prime concern.

Wilder played the alcoholic Waco Kid in **Blazing Saddles** and then went on to star in Brooks' best and most disciplined picture, **Young Frankenstein** (1974), shot in black and white, which used many of the original settings from Universal's Thirties Frankenstein films and which sent up the original James Whale picture with transparent affection. Anachronism was the key here rather than a rude explosion of the traditions of the horror film, and the character of the demented scientist gave Gene Wilder a fresh license for his rages. Meanwhile Peter Boyle was genuinely touching as the Creature who longs to don white tie and tails and dance "Puttin' on the Ritz" with his creator.

Silent Movie (1976) (in which the only spoken word falls from the lips of the great French mime Marcel Marceau) and **High Anxiety** (1977), a spoof of Hitchcock set-pieces that probably looked a lot better on paper than it does on celluloid, completed a quartet of films that fed off other films. Thereafter Brooks moved on to a no less controversial field of comedy with **History of the World Part I** (1981) and became a serious behind-the-scenes patron-producer with **The Elephant Man** (1980).

Mel Brooks' **Blazing Saddles** (1973) was the commercial breakthrough film for the gloriously unstable writer-director of **The Producers** (1968). Guying the traditions and clichés of the Western, it starred Gene Wilder as the Waco Kid and Cleavon Little as the West's first black sheriff. In the film's madcap finale the pair accidentally (and anachronistically) gatecrash a film studio where a big musical production number is being filmed.

"I look at my films," said Mel Brooks, "and I think, 'Am I *that* vulgar, *that* Jewish?' And the answer is, 'Yes.' You can only be your true self in a film these days. I give you myself; you give me the price of admission. That's the deal."

Brooks' career without Wilder (they parted company after **Young Frankenstein**) continued in robust overdrive, but the actor's sputtered and stalled when he turned to direction with **The Adventure of Sherlock Holmes's Smarter Brother** (1975) and **The World's Greatest Lover** (1977) (which pounded the same beat as **Silent Movie**). Yet his performances continued to impress, especially in the railroad train thriller **Silver Streak** (1976) and opposite Harrison Ford in **The Frisco Kid** (1979).

The Seventies had seen comedy become a far more direct and personal statement: the knotty problems of relationships were now the banana skins and verbal abuse replaced the custard pie. The key figures in the predominantly Jewish comedy of the decade gave us reflections of themselves in their work, however risky that initially seemed in terms of acceptability by a public bred on mechanical comic formulas.

Above and top: *Made in black and white and utilizing the set designed for the 1931 James Whale original,* **Young Frankenstein** *(1974) presented Mel Brooks at his least frantic and most film-reverent. Gene Wilder was the new-generation resurrectionist, Peter Boyle his gauche creature and the late Marty Feldman the requisite lab assistant who can't be trusted to use his brains.*

Right: *The third of Mel Brooks' four Hollywood spoofs,* **Silent Movie** *(1976) was a picture with only one word of dialogue (and, perversely, that is spoken by the French mime Marcel Marceau). The film gave a starring role to a manic stalwart of the Brooks repertory company, Dom DeLuise.*

6 Months Dead

The Sounds of Music

Chapter 4

The metamorphosis of the movie musical in the Seventies was brought about by two major factors. The first recognized the vital importance of aiming films at young audiences; the second was governed by the sudden awakening of the record industry to the commercial potential of the soundtrack album.

Few film genres had divided the generations as sharply as the musical. The young could hardly sit still through the theatrical and absurdly romanticized posturing of the two-dimensional shows-on-celluloid that had passed for film musicals in the previous decades. Typical examples include film versions of such Rodgers and Hammerstein stage classics as **Oklahoma!** (1955), **Carousel** (1956) and **The King and I** (1956), which represented everything that was middle-aged and middle-class about the movies. Teenagers would rather stay at home and listen to the radio or watch television than accompany their elders to the cinema. And they had a new beat to which to tap their toes: in the very year that Deborah Kerr's governess was teaching Yul Brynner's Siamese monarch to polka, the kiss-curled Bill Haley erupted on to the cinema screens in the crudely made but topical exploitation movie **Rock Around the Clock** (1956). While one generation was sighing wistfully and humming tunes from Broadway, the next was rocking in the aisles to a more urgent beat.

The young audience, abruptly separated from their parents, soon found new idols and new totems that became part and parcel of the rock revolution. Marlon Brando's nihilistic bike boy in **The Wild One** (1954); the sexually suggestive gyrations of Elvis Presley, already denounced by elders and clergy as the Devil's own tool; the violent frustration of James Dean — who never had the slightest connection with the rock movement in movies himself, but who nevertheless became emblematic of the age once he put away his flecked sports jacket, changed into a red windcheater and blue Levis, kicked his motorcycle boot through a family oil painting and went to the bad in **Rebel Without a Cause** (1955).

Right: *"An Aquarian exposition of love and peace" — that's how the half-million young people who gathered on Max Yasgur's New York State dairy farm liked to think of the Woodstock Music and Art Fair. Director Michael Wadleigh was there with 20 cameramen and eight assistants to record the musicians and the audience they played for in **Woodstock** (1970), a three-hour-plus documentary that made striking use of split-screen techniques.*

A king is born

If the waltzes of the traditional film composers pleased the ear, rock's appeal was more primitively to the loins. The real astonishment was that there were so few bona fide movies celebrating the new music. The teenage audience had fallen away, finding live rock more exciting than the cinema and prepared to hunt it down on radio and television, at theaters and in clubs.

The cinema had yet to discover that young filmgoers were to be of such strategic importance to its commercial future and made only token attempts to woo them. However, the phenomenon of Elvis Presley's success was such that not even a near-comatose musical cinema could ignore him entirely. He was rushed into a Western, **Love Me Tender** (1956), and then given one of the few decent musicals in his fifteen-year movie career, **Loving You** (1957), in which he had to make do with a creaking plot about a young working-class boy who makes good in showbusiness with an unfashionably raucous music. At least this paper-thin plot gave Elvis the chance to be himself which, at that time, was all the fans asked of him on screen. Subsequently Hollywood producers altered, laundered and sanitized him. They did everything *but* what was needed: to let him be. With its traditional fear of new things, Hollywood wasted

a golden opportunity: in tampering with the new wine and decanting it into old bottles, they failed to take full advantage of a growing market.

Relieved to see their caution seemingly vindicated by rock's often feeble impact on the box-office, producers turned again to the traditional musical and must have breathed a sigh of genuine and enormous relief when **The Sound of Music** (1965), the most surefire of the Rodgers and Hammerstein confections, combined nuns and children in a sugary mix to create a monster hit. But that film emptied the Rodgers and Hammerstein coffers, so the same star (the newly Oscar-sanctioned Julie Andrews) and the same director, Robert Wise, were pressed into service for **Star!** (1968), a musical biography of Gertrude Lawrence. The sound of its resounding belly flop is one that still echoes in the ears of the middle-aged Fox board who sanctioned it.

Above: *The "phenomenon of innocence" that was Woodstock soon took a nasty knock at the Altamont concert where a spectator died at the hands of Hell's Angels while the Rolling Stones played on. David and Albert Maysles' and Charlotte Zwerin's* **Gimme Shelter** *(1970) became a chronicle of the times as much as a music documentary.*

Right: *In **Woodstock** (1970), ex-Lovin' Spoonful guitarist John Sebastian sang "I Had a Dream", laced his rap with a few trendy obscenities and proved a crowd-pleaser. The group's big hits (1966) had been "Daydream" and "Summer in the City", their only US no. 1.*

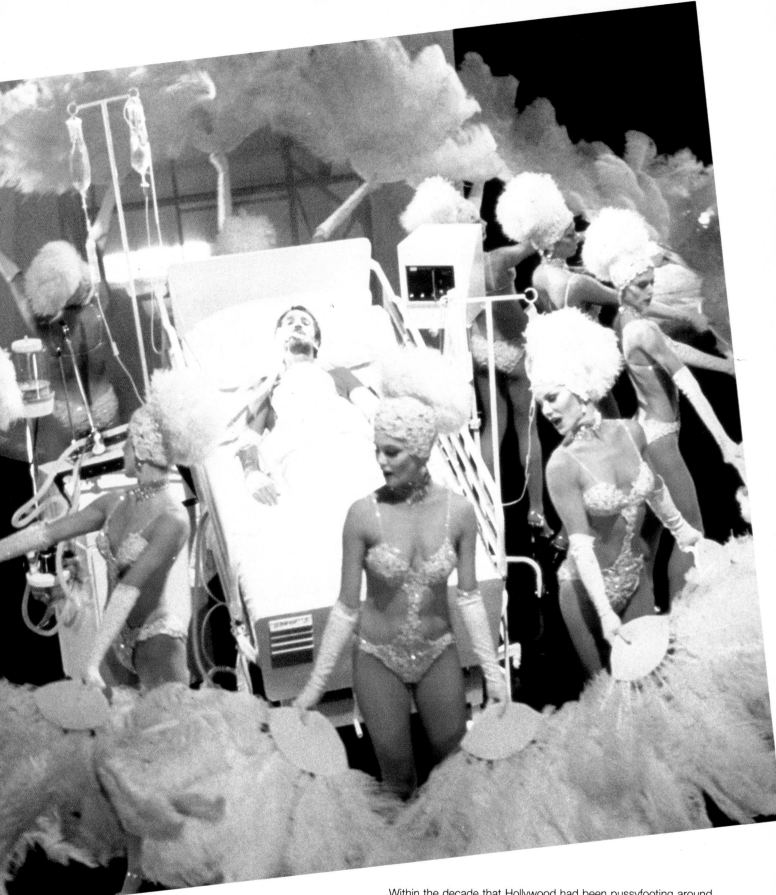

Left and above: *Bob Fosse's partly autobiographical, self-indulgent but occasionally brilliant musical* **All That Jazz** *(1979) had a Fellini-like vision of the life and death of a top choreographer (Roy Scheider). A strange but potent cocktail of whiplash choreography, erotica and open-heart surgery, it concludes with the apposite production number, "Bye, Bye Love(Life)".*

Within the decade that Hollywood had been pussyfooting around the vexed question of the musical, another generation, once newly enfranchised teenagers of the James Dean—Bill Haley—Elvis Presley years, had come to eminence in the film and music industries. They were deft in their assessments and had the confident certainty to act according to their own tastes. While the conventional musical became more sporadic in appearance and more elephantine in budget (**Hello, Dolly!** (1969) and **Camelot** (1967) were the more

successful of these years), younger producers placed their fingers on the cinema's pulse and issued an instant diagnosis: modern music was a certain bait to lure the truant teenage audience back into the movie houses.

The Stones play on

The significant breakthrough film was Michael Wadleigh's **Woodstock** (1970), which became a box-office champion despite being not only a documentary but one which lasted for three hours. It was not the social phenomenon of teenage tribes in peaceful coexistence that brought the young audience back into the cinema: it was the opportunity to see and hear their favorite groups and bands. Building

on that success was **Gimme Shelter** (1970), which recorded the Altamont concert at which the short-lived Woodstock spirit died, along with the music lover stabbed by Hell's Angels as the Rolling Stones played on and the cameras rolled. Concert documentaries proliferated: **Monterey Pop** (1969), **Keep on Rockin'** (1973) and **Wattstax** (1973) were three of the most notable, while a more ambitious documentary, **Let the Good Times Roll** (1973), yoked the musical phenomenon to the wider social one of the youth explosion with a clever and frequently witty use of split-screen photography, sometimes showing contemporary rock stars performing alongside their younger selves.

Now that rock had been embraced by the movie Establishment, the floodgates were open to the tide of modern operas that were enjoying theatrical success. Though most of the output of the prolific Andrew Lloyd Webber has been astutely held back from the cinema,

Left: *Director Norman Jewison took the Andrew Lloyd Webber-Tim Rice rock opera* **Jesus Christ Superstar** *(1973) out on to Israeli desert locations, but the film never found a satisfactory style to match up with the driving energy of the music. Ted Neeley played Jesus, and Hawaiian-born Yvonne Elliman (not shown), Eric Clapton's sometime backing vocalist, made an impression as Mary Magdalene with "I Don't Know How to Love Him".*

Right: *A rock Gospel According to Saint Matthew, David Greene's* **Godspell** *(1973) derived from a successful stage show. David Haskell played a brightly dressed character who was a compression of John the Baptist ("I wanna get washed up," says the clown-garbed Jesus of Victor Garber when Haskell turns up at the fountain in Central Park) and Judas Iscariot.*

Above: *In his lively film of the Who's rock opera* **Tommy** *(1975), Ken Russell invented the frantic style of today's video promo. Roger Daltrey played the deaf, dumb and blind messiah and Ann-Margret played his faithless mother.*

director Norman Jewison was able to undertake a full-blooded film version of **Jesus Christ Superstar** (1973), set in Israeli desert locations and offering a petulant, flaxen-haired Jesus in Ted Neeley but electrified by the performance of Carl Anderson as Judas Iscariot. The other opera in which religion went pop was **Godspell** (1973), which reached the screen in a version by David Greene that invited almost universal calumny though it seemed a fair, even inventive, account of the stage version. **Catch My Soul** (1974), a modern-dress version of Shakespeare's *Othello* directed by the unpredictable Patrick McGoohan, fared little better and the genre had to look for its salvation to a British director who was now lauded for doing all the very things that had previously brought him into disrepute.

One could say that Ken Russell had been making musicals from the very beginnings of his varied career in television and movies. His biographies of classical composers and artists were marked by fanciful touches, wild extravagances and breaches of taste that often appalled. Where some audiences looked for gentle chamber music, he played the most wayward and experimental of operas – with the volume at full blast. But when he turned his attention to **Tommy** (1975), a rock opera that had been performed on record and in concert by the British band The Who, he suddenly had full license (indeed full need) of all his visual extravagances. Tommy (Roger Daltrey) is a deaf, dumb and blind boy who has been reduced to his near-catatonic condition by the trauma of seeing his father murdered

Left: *In **Tommy** (1975), the "deaf, dumb and blind kid" is tormented by his cousin Kevin (Paul Nicholas). With cousins like that, who needs brothers and sisters?*

Right: *Horribly disfigured, his head caught in a record-pressing machine, the masked hero (William Finley) of Brian De Palma's **Phantom of the Paradise** (1974) lives on, a voiceless mutilation, to haunt the 24-hour rock palace of the title and to supervise the career of a girl singer whom he adores from the touchline.*

Below: *Tim Curry played the "sweet transvestite from transsexual Transylvania" in **The Rocky Horror Picture Show** (1975), a musical that became a camp cult success. Jim Sharman directed, from Richard O'Brien's script.*

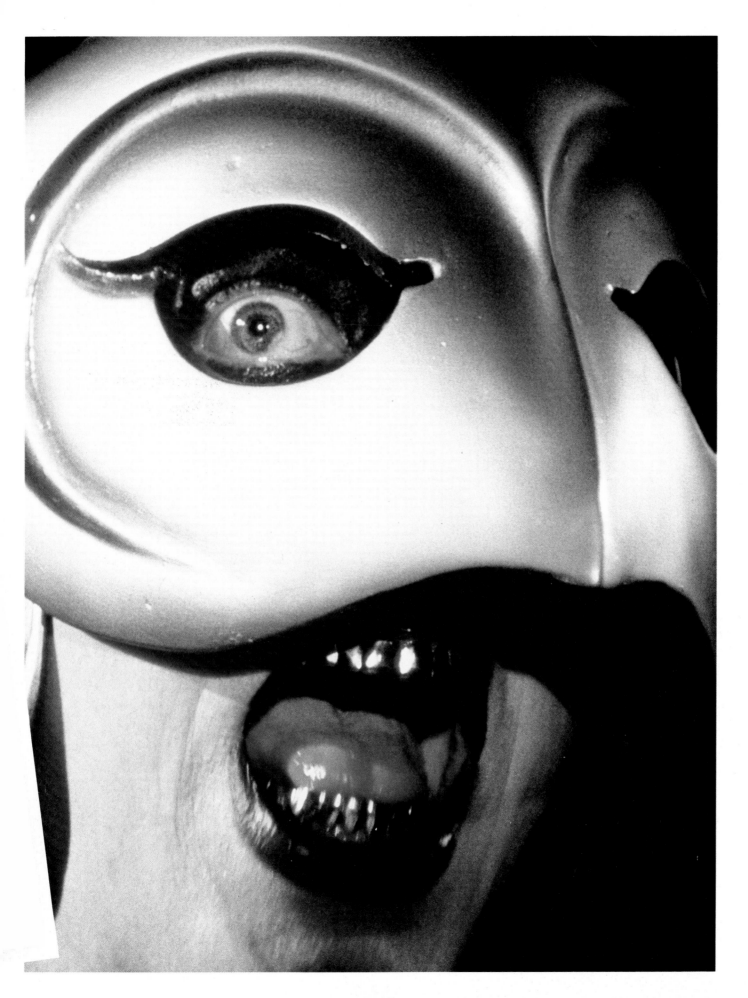

by his mother's lover. His liberation, rise and fall as a wizard of the pinball tables and a marketable messiah gave Russell all the scope he could have wished for in striking out at sacred cows. The cinema exposed great yawning gaps in the narrative, cracks which Russell papered over with panache. The film, a true opera with *every* word being sung, was really the forerunner of today's pop video promo.

Gothic rock

The rock musical around which a still extant cult grew was **The Rocky Horror Picture Show** (1975), an unbridled fantasy about an androgynous intergalactic emissary (a role created with impudent brio by Tim Curry) passing the time making creatures for his/her sexual gratification. Into the Gothic castle-den of this "sweet transvestite from transsexual Transylvania" stumble the hapless Brad and Janet (Barry Bostwick and Susan Sarandon) to become entrapped in the nightmare hobbies of Mr Curry. The film clearly has a compulsive "see-again" effect upon sections of its audience, many of whom dress up as the characters and attend midnight screenings at which a duplicate cast arranges itself on the stage and plays out each scene in accompaniment to the celluloid counterparts. This phenomenon emerged in New York, but its documentation in Alan Parker's musical **Fame** (1980) caused imitations in many other countries.

The same air of barely suppressed hysteria attaches to Brian De Palma's **Phantom of the Paradise** (1974), supposedly a rock version of **The Phantom of the Opera** but in fact a satirical fusion of elements of *Faust*, **Frankenstein** and **The Picture of Dorian Gray** as well. Paul Williams, who also wrote the pounding score, plays Swan, the ever-youthful head of Death Records, pledged to contract new souls for his Satanic master. Swan's own earthly instincts are to pirate a new rock cantata written by Winslow Leach (William Finley) and use it to open his 24-hour rock palace, The Paradise. A vengeful Leach gets his head caught in a record-pressing machine and lives on, a voiceless disfiguration, to haunt The Paradise and covertly to supervise the career of an adored girl singer. This part is true to the original, but the climactic orgy of coast-to-coast televised massacre and mayhem as Leach brings a final revenge to purge his soul, are pure De Palma, scenes in which can easily be recognized the excesses of a director who was to make such extreme movies as **Dressed to Kill** (1980), **Scarface** (1983) and **Body Double** (1984).

The traditional musical was barely getting a look in during this period. Elvis Presley had finally admitted the paucity of his own screen material and allowed documentarists to record his electric stage performances in **Elvis, That's the Way It Is** (1970) and **Elvis on Tour** (1972), which were, sadly, to be his last two films. Barbra Streisand asked him to star opposite her in yet another remake of **A Star is Born** (1976), but when Elvis proved unwilling to commit himself, she went ahead with the rock-oriented revision with Kris Kristofferson as the burned-out singer whose career is eclipsed by that of his girlfriend.

Right: *Czech-born director Milos Forman had scored impressively with two American films, **Taking Off** (1971) and **One Flew Over the Cuckoo's Nest** (1975), before he turned his attention to the musical **Hair**. It was rigorously anti-Vietnam, vigorously anti-authority (this is Treat Williams dancing on the dinner table), but still played very much like the Sixties hippie period piece it had already become when it was belatedly made in 1979. Galt MacDermot wrote the music, including the popular "Aquarius".*

Top right: *Alan Parker's celebration of youthful optimism, **Fame** (1980), put the New York High School for the Performing Arts on the map, sired a television series and briefly made a star out of the unknown Irene Cara.*

80

Left and far left: *In the third version (1976) of **A Star Is Born** (fourth if you count the 1932 **What Price Hollywood?**) and the most crass, Barbra Streisand turned the heavy-duty Hollywood story into an egomaniac love feast with herself as the singer on the way up and Kris Kristofferson as the one in decline. One critic called it "A Bore Is Starred": certainly it represented the high-water mark of Streisand's self-absorption.*

Below: *This scene from **The Wiz** (1978) would have come as a shock to L. Frank Baum, who published The Wonderful Wizard of Oz in 1900 and followed it with thirteen further Oz books. Even Judy Garland might have had difficulty in recognizing the soporific poppy fields, transformed into Poppy Street, where ladies of easy virtue peddle coke.*

Streisand had remained a potent box-office force in the Seventies, but, although her recording career continued in top gear, she was rarely cast in screen musicals. Neither **Hello, Dolly!** nor **On a Clear Day You Can See Forever** (1970) lived up to the box-office hopes held for them and **Funny Lady** (1975), a belated sequel to her Oscar-winning debut in **Funny Girl** (1968), remained only her second musical of the decade until **A Star is Born**.

Dance fever

The musical emphasis began shifting from song to dance. Health awareness and exercise faddism had driven people in huge numbers to gyms and the new aerobic classes, where a fresh appreciation of dance was gained. Twyla Tharp's choreography for **Hair** (1979), the oddly belated film Milos Forman made of the 1960s stage hit, was one of its strongest selling points. The only Broadway musical that was solidly on Hollywood's books was the dance-centered *A Chorus Line*, which, though seriously considered by such directors as Sidney Lumet and Mike Nichols, did not reach the screen for another decade when Richard Attenborough helmed the project.

The Turning Point (1977) celebrates classical dance, featuring the talented, youthful ballet star Mikhail Baryshnikov, while modern dance is represented by Alan Parker's popular study of young people

Left: *Sidney Lumet's all-black musical, **The Wiz** (1978), cast Diana Ross as Dorothy Gale, befriended by Michael Jackson (Scarecrow), Nipsey Russell (Tinman) and Ted Ross (Lion) on the yellow brick road to Oz.*

Bottom far left: ***The Turning Point** (1977) features emigré dancer Mikhail Baryshnikov as a fickle Russian stud and Leslie Browne as the ballerina he toys with.*

Below: *Bob Fosse's **Cabaret** (1972) was perhaps the best musical of the Seventies, an intelligent reworking for the cinema (carefully cast and zingingly choreographed) of the Kander and Ebb show, itself derived from Christopher Isherwood's writings about decadent life in pre-war Berlin. Liza Minnelli as the singer Sally Bowles, Joel Grey as the effetely dangerous MC, lighting cameraman Geoffrey Unsworth and director Fosse all richly deserved their Oscars.*

Below: *After small roles in **The Devil's Rain** (1975) and **Carrie** (1976), John Travolta sprang to stardom in **Saturday Night Fever*** *(1977) as Tony Manero, the disco-dancing young Brooklynite brought to heel by love of a good girl (Karen Lynn Gorney, not shown). It owed its success to more than the expert marketing of its star-studded soundtrack: under John Badham's tight direction it emerged as an engrossing study of the rites of passage of the working-class American male.*

Right: *The ascendant star of John Travolta (right) carried* **Grease** *(1978) into orbit. An inflated Broadway musical about Fifties teenagers, it derived great box-office benefit from the casting of Travolta as Danny Zuko, the greaser with a heart of gold who falls for Sandra Dee clone Olivia Newton-John (not shown).*

at the School for the Performing Arts in New York. **Fame** not only sired a successful television series but ushered in a series of youth-geared musicals that had dance as their theme. **Saturday Night Fever** explained in salty language the tribal rites of the new Saturday night, but also spotlighted tellingly the universal obsession with disco dancing, an art demonstrated brilliantly by John Travolta, who had hitherto been seen only in supporting roles in **The Devil's Rain** (1975) and Brian De Palma's **Carrie** (1976). The teaming of Travolta and Olivia Newton-John was repeated in **Grease**, a nostalgic return to the simplicity of high-school life in the Fifties which was a huge commercial success. But when the couple subsequently went their separate ways, Travolta into the ineffectual **Moment by Moment** (1978) and Newton-John into the dire roller-skating disco musical **Xanadu** (1980), popularity deserted them.

Much of the impact of **Saturday Night Fever** derived from the comparably huge sales achieved by the soundtrack album made by The Bee Gees and other (non-appearing) musicians. The record industry's tardy admission that there was a symbiotic relationship between film and album was of signal importance. Before the Seventies, only a musical with a proven stage pedigree, a **South Pacific** (1958) or a **Carousel**, could expect to notch up significant soundtrack album sales. Furthermore, because of contractual difficulties and the unwillingness of the record business tycoons to simplify or circumvent them, film producers were tied to the commissioning of original music for their scores.

Dennis Hopper and Peter Fonda in **Easy Rider** decided to accompany their images of young people on the road with the very sounds that those hippies listened to, the top chart sounds of the day, not some monotonous score by a studio-retained composer. Although the accompanying soundtrack album was delayed while legal knots were untied (the scale of the film's success was a virtual guarantee of comparable album sales), the exercise pioneered the way for a new approach to music in the movies.

Thereafter films like George Lucas's **American Graffiti** (1973) evoked precise moments in time by the unfettered use of a musical shorthand, and the accompanying albums became more and more an essential part of the film's marketing strategy. The day was not far away when such an album was a prerequisite, sometimes the *raison d'être* of a film, even a non-musical film. This trend reached its nadir in the Eighties.

The Lady is a Champ

Chapter 5

Although a film like Paul Mazursky's **An Unmarried Woman** (1977) reveals its subject and the dynamics of its plot in its very title, the dilemmas faced by Jill Clayburgh – one of Hollywood's most likeable, strongest actresses during the Seventies – are presented in a romantic but fundamentally truthful light. Clayburgh's character, Erica, is unmarried only temporarily in that her successful, wealthy husband of seventeen years has just left her for a girl he met while buying a shirt in Bloomingdale's. The film shows Erica coming to terms with the break-up by revising her opinions of herself, redefining that self in its own right rather than as an extension of somebody else's personality, and finally going out with another man.

The difference between Mazursky's film and romantic comedies from previous decades lies, however, in Erica's refusal to drop everything for Alan Bates' abstract expressionist painter simply out of love for him or because he expects her to. It is not so much loneliness that is her problem, as the problems that men, flitting around this newly "available" woman like moths round a flame, bring to her sense of independence.

Women's rights

The movement in feminism and Women's Liberation was one of the major social issues of the Seventies once the radical image of bra-burning softened and women of every walk of life started to reflect on and to identify with the political thinking which argued that one half of the population had rights equal to the other. In short, that women were people too, that they deserved the same rights and considerations already given to sexual, social, political and ethnic minorities.

Liza Minnelli, in Martin Scorsese's **New York, New York** (1977), chooses her career when a fork in her life suggests a choice has to be made between showbusiness or a brutalizing life with her husband (Robert De Niro). And when Neil Simon uses the self-sacrificing finale of the old-fashionedly romantic **Casablanca** in his droll spoof **The Cheap Detective** (with Louise Fletcher standing in for Ingrid Bergman), Nicol Williamson has the right riposte: "What a brave, beautiful, extremely boring woman," he says.

But, as feminism bubbled under everyday lives that were slow to change, it became difficult for writers to pin down a woman's social role. And because some of the early liberationists were thought to be grim and joyless, confirming the worst fears of those opposed to the movement, a movie on the very subject of equality and independence might have tended to plunge into turgid introspection.

Right: *Jill Clayburgh played the emerging feminist of Paul Mazursky's* **An Unmarried Woman** *(1978) who, abandoned by her husband, discovers a new set of priorities in the relationship she subsequently establishes with a successful painter (Alan Bates).*

Women bewailed the fact that they would never see faithful images of themselves reflected on the screen while the Hollywood writing Establishment continued to be male-dominated. Ironically, however, it was a man, Robert Getchell, who penned the breakthrough film, Martin Scorsese's **Alice Doesn't Live Here Anymore** (1975), in which Ellen Burstyn gave an Oscar-winning performance. Alice gave up her dreams of becoming a singer at the age of nineteen for marriage and motherhood. But, abruptly widowed at thirty-two, she picks up the threads, leaves the stifling town of her less-than-perfect marriage and sets off with her son for Monterey, where her abandoned career once looked hopeful. Along the way she suffers the fate of a single woman being exploited by men, before meeting, as happens in Clayburgh's **An Unmarried Woman**, a potential dream lover in Kris Kristofferson. And here too, it is the man who is forced to consider giving up his lifestyle, allowing his new partner to pursue her much sought-after freedom.

Sex change

The star actresses of the Seventies were far from the traditional idea of stereotyped beauty: Streisand and Minnelli in the acting-singing stakes; Burstyn, Fletcher and Clayburgh. The beauties of the previous decades, hour-glass figures with what were presented as second-hand brains, were rejected, possibly by a predominantly female audience. Research shows that more women were attending the cinema at this time than men, and also that it tended to be the woman who chose the movie for the occasional family outing. Clearly they voted out Raquel Welch and Ursula Andress, preferring to watch more realistic versions of womanhood. Another response to this phenomenon was the mushrooming in the early Seventies of the buddy movies, in which male-bonding replaced the traditional boy-girl romance. Mostly these were not even implicitly homosexual in tone, but merely helped to fill the blank which might have been filled by movies tackling the plight of confused women in search of a role.

Once, when asked why there were no good parts being written for women, Shirley MacLaine replied with more than a grain of truth that

Bottom and right: *In* **New York, New York** *(1977), director Martin Scorsese cast Liza Minnelli as the singer whose career eclipses that of her volatile saxophonist husband (Robert De Niro). The theme owes much to* **A Star is Born** *and, as though in homage to the 1954 version starring Minnelli's mother, Judy Garland, there is a mammoth production number, "Happy Endings", that pays tribute to* **Star***'s "Born in a Trunk".*

Below: *Ellen Burstyn (not shown) was the Oscar-winning Alice of* **Alice Doesn't Live Here Anymore** *(1975). Part of her liberation and rebirth takes place in the Tucson cafe where she has to conquer the hostility of a prickly fellow waitress (Diane Ladd, right) and also to sort out her own feelings towards the young farmer (Kris Kristofferson, left) who makes a play for Alice herself.*

89

there were. It was just that they were all being played by Robert Redford. But gradually the wheel turned and the Paul Newman–Robert Redford partnership, so successful in **Butch Cassidy and the Sundance Kid** that it was repeated in **The Sting** (1973), gave way to a climate in which roles usually reserved for men were often rethought for star actresses. After the Oscar-earning impact of her performance in **One Flew Over the Cuckoo's Nest** (1975), Louise Fletcher won the role of a psychiatrist in John Boorman's **Exorcist II: The Heretic** (1977) from a male contender.

By the mid-Seventies the buddy movies had abated (not before they had seen some admirable teamings: Warren Beatty and Jack Nicholson in **The Fortune** (1975), Clint Eastwood and Jeff Bridges in **Thunderbolt and Lightfoot** (1974), Steve McQueen and Dustin Hoffman in **Papillon** (1973)). A "male" picture had meant action, excitement and adventure with absolutely no restrictions of genre or location; by the same token a "female" picture would be assumed to be set in the home or in a convent. That thinking was grimly satirized in Ira Levin's novel (and Bryan Forbes' film, adapted by William Goldman) **The Stepford Wives** (1975), in which a coven of Ivy League husbands robotize their wives into loyal domestic drudges without a thought in their computerized heads. The Playboy fantasy had become a living nightmare and, in the central role, Katharine Ross earned a quietly satisfying revenge for being the relatively marginal "love interest" in **Butch Cassidy and the Sundance Kid**.

In Michael Ritchie's football comedy, **Semi-Tough**, Jill Clayburgh lives in contented asexuality with team members Burt Reynolds and Kris Kristofferson, to the dismay of her father (Robert Preston), the manager, who thinks the lack of sexual activity within the *ménage à trois* reflects embarrassingly on his players' masculinity: this modern thinking and sexual freedom from stereotypes simply makes the men appear gay. Preston's fears, however, are allayed when Clayburgh

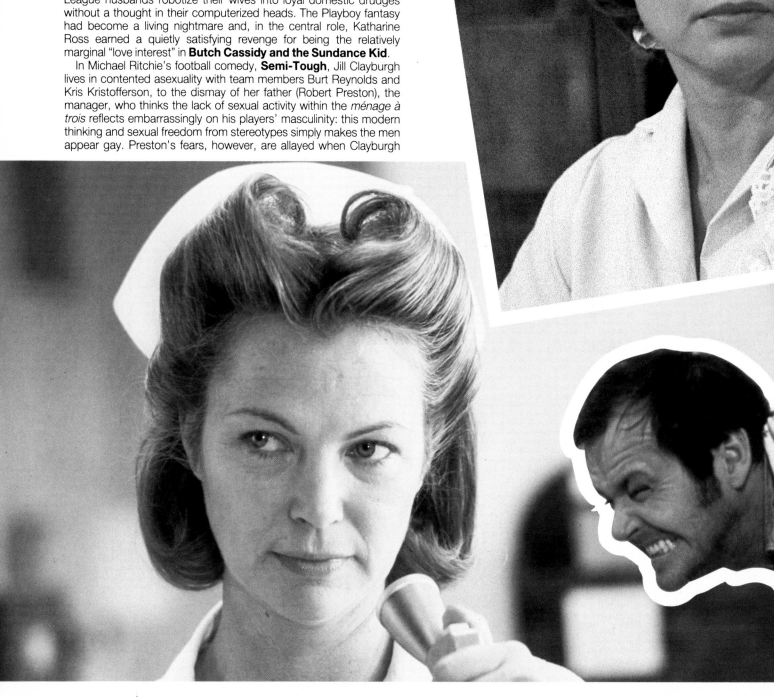

Left: *Maybe Alice (Ellen Burstyn), a hashhouse waitress in Tucson in* **Alice Doesn't Live Here Anymore** *(1974), will never get to Monterey to resume her long-gone singing career. Maybe she has found the love of a good man — at least he knocks seven shades of daylight out of her appalling son (a Mott the Hoople fan!), so he can't be all bad. But at least she gets to make the choice — and director Martin Scorsese carries on his love/hate relationship with American male chauvinism (slightly constrained by Robert Getchell's script). Burstyn deservedly won an Oscar.*

Below: *For years Kirk Douglas owned the rights to Ken Kesey's 1962 novel* **One Flew Over the Cuckoo's Nest** *and, when he grew too old to play the rebellious McMurphy, passed the project on to his actor/producer son Michael, who cast Jack Nicholson in the role. Louise Fletcher* **(below far left)** *was outstanding as the loathsome Nurse Ratched who works in the asylum in which McMurphy is incarcerated. Milos Forman directed and they all took Oscars in 1975.*

falls for Kristofferson, surrendering her mental independence as she follows him into a fashionable but bizarre alternative therapy group. The conventional happy ending, complete with wedding ceremony, is fortunately ditched by Ritchie along with Kristofferson, who jilts his bride-to-be at the altar and leaves her to rediscover herself and her happiness in a possibly platonic relationship with the more down-to-earth Reynolds.

Male stereotypes were also the concern of Hal Ashby's **Coming Home** (1978), in which Jane Fonda played an ordinary young Army wife who sees her husband (Bruce Dern) off for a tour of duty in Vietnam and then occupies the time on her hands by working with war veterans in a local hospital. There she meets and falls in love with a young paraplegic (Jon Voight) and finds tender love and sexual satisfaction for the first time in her life. Dern's return from the war, his emotions all the more frozen by months of all-male mess hall camaraderie, brings about the thorough questioning by women of the image of macho virility.

Good girl, bad girl

The question of a woman's unashamed sexual appetite was tackled in **Looking for Mr Goodbar** (1977), which dared to suggest that the madonna and the whore might coexist happily within the same woman, albeit to male irritation and perplexity. Diane Keaton, in her most demanding role away from Woody Allen, played a girl who was a saintly teacher by day and a sexually cruising barfly by night. Having

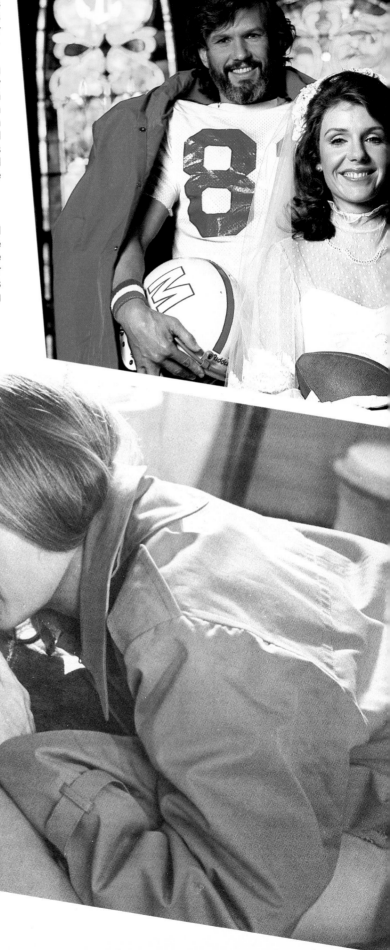

Left: Michael Ritchie's amusing satire, **Semi-Tough** (1977), revolved around a ménage à trois of two footballers (Burt Reynolds, right, and Kris Kristofferson) and their manager's daughter (Jill Clayburgh). A multiple divorcée, she nearly marries Kris Kristofferson, but at the last moment ....

Bottom far left: Starting Over (1979), Alan J. Pakula's wise, barbed comedy of personal relationships, starred the persistently underrated Burt Reynolds as an attractive middle-aged man who suffers a crisis of confidence when ditched by his ambitious singer wife (Candice Bergen, pictured, who effortlessly stole the picture) until he begins to forge a new relationship with an equally insecure teacher, played by Jill Clayburgh. But when the wife attempts a reconciliation – seduction followed by a truly excruciating song she has composed for him – he realizes where his loyalty lies.

Below: One of the best of the "buddy" movies, Michael Cimino's **Thunderbolt and Lightfoot** (1974) starred Clint Eastwood as a criminal (initially disguised as a preacher!) in search of loot from an earlier robbery that has gone missing while he was in jail. Jeff Bridges was the young drifter with whom he falls into step. The drag sported by Bridges is worn merely that he might work more distractingly as a decoy in a bullion robbery.

had herself sterilized for fear of transmitting a genetic disability, she no longer cares for the uses and abuses of her own body, and her increasingly risky nocturnal escapades (the danger is a part of the fatal attraction) end in her brutal, undeserved murder at the hands of one of her pick-ups.

The theme of career versus maternity was seldom more handsomely presented than in Herbert Ross' **The Turning Point**, in which Shirley MacLaine plays a woman who gave up her dancing career for marriage and motherhood and Anne Bancroft plays the best friend who pulled down the emotional shutters to become a star, while also being godmother to MacLaine's daughter who is herself at a similar crossroads in her own womanhood.

In Fred Zinnemann's **Julia** (1977), the theme was the laying down in childhood of friendship bonds that will make inexorable demands in adult life. Jane Fonda played the writer Lillian Hellman fulfilled by her own career success and a strong relationship with fellow author Dashiell Hammett (Jason Robards Jnr). Vanessa Redgrave played Julia, a woman whose safety is put at physical risk by her political

commitments. The bonds between them are so strong that Lillian has no option but to help, to halt her career and relationship midflow, when Julia is in danger. The film was notable in showing the intensity of a female friendship while pointing out its platonic nature. When a lout has the gall to suggest that the relationship *must* be sexual to be

Above inset: In **Looking for Mr Goodbar** (1977), Diane Keaton plays a teacher who cruises the singles bars by night and is murdered by one of her pick-ups. Richard Brooks' film includes an early performance by Richard Gere as one of Keaton's conquests.

Top: Which of the characters is **Semi-Tough** in the 1977 comedy? Shake (Kris Kristofferson) is semi-tough enough to stand up Barbara Jane (Jill Clayburgh) at the altar, using his est (here called B.E.A.T.) training — and she, though unmoved by this self-realization therapy, is semi-tough enough to take it and find consolation with another footballer ....

Right: *Hal Ashby's* **Coming Home** *won 1978 Oscars for both Jon Voight as the Vietvet paraplegic and Jane Fonda as the married woman whose love affair with him alters her notions of manliness.*

Above: *The timeless career-versus-marriage dichotomy was debated in **The Turning Point**, a handsome 1977 movie set against a background of classical dance. Anne Bancroft (right) was the ballerina who gave up love and marriage for the stage; Shirley MacLaine (left) the lifelong friend who sacrificed fame for domesticity.*

that close, Lillian rounds on him and knocks him off his chair, a moment that the audience is often moved to cheer.

But, by the end of the decade, the novelty of feminism as a brightly signposted theme was wearing off and gender was altogether less of a factor in casting. As Garbo had said as **Ninotchka** (1939), the Russian envoy sent to Paris to investigate the misdemeanors of the male members of the trade delegation, "Don't make an issue of my womanhood." The movies were finally taking her at her word, though sexist attitudes were still tersely corrected in such films as **Coma** (1978) with Geneviève Bujold as a female doctor battling against a male-dominated medical conspiracy.

Fred Zinnemann's **Julia** (1977) was based on the (more or less) true story of a friendship laid down in girlhood that makes irresistible demands in later years. Jane Fonda played the author Lillian Hellman who finds herself compelled temporarily to jettison her affair with author Dashiell Hammett and her own writing career to help Julia (played by Vanessa Redgrave) when the latter's political activities place her life in danger before World War II.

Bigotry, brutality and the backlash

As women took up key roles in industry and politics, there was a predictable male backlash. It was no longer possible to smile condescendingly at the idea of a woman holding down a job while running the home: millions of women were successfully doing just that and, when the two jobs did prove incompatible, sometimes they left the domestic chores to their husbands. The sexual assertiveness and apparent threat to men's employment opportunities posed by liberated women fed a grass-roots appetite for filmic revenge.

While the end of the decade saw Jane Fonda, Lily Tomlin and Dolly Parton getting their own back on a chauvinist boss (Dabney Coleman) in the black office comedy **Nine to Five** (1980) — with its violent imagery wrapped in sheer farce — the male reaction was less subtle.

Violent and fundamentally sexist thrillers like Brian De Palma's **Dressed to Kill** inspired women to protest and picket cinemas, though it could be argued that this particular example was no more than a hothouse version of Alfred Hitchcock's **Psycho** (1960), which, twenty years earlier, had offered a sacrificial female victim in the cinema's most celebrated murder. But other horror shockers demonstrated an unmistakable misogyny. The terrorizing, humiliation, murder and mutilation of women alone became a recurring theme in such "stalk and slash" movies as **When a Stranger Calls** (1979) and **He Knows You're Alone** (1980).

In each of these films lies the suggestion that the baton of avenging violence is passed from hand to male hand. You have only to accept

Top left: *A superb performance by Jane Fonda (rewarded by an Oscar) lies at the heart of **Klute** (1971), a murder mystery that was only the second film as director by former producer Alan J. Pakula. The eponymous private detective is played by Donald Sutherland but the film really scores with the gutsy, modern and brilliantly sustained characterization of the high-class call girl, Bree Daniels, who unwittingly places herself at risk when Klute starts stirring up the muddy waters that are settling over a recent murder case.*

Right: *Jane Fonda and Jason Robards as writers and lovers Lillian Hellman and Dashiell Hammett in Fred Zinnemann's **Julia** (1977).*

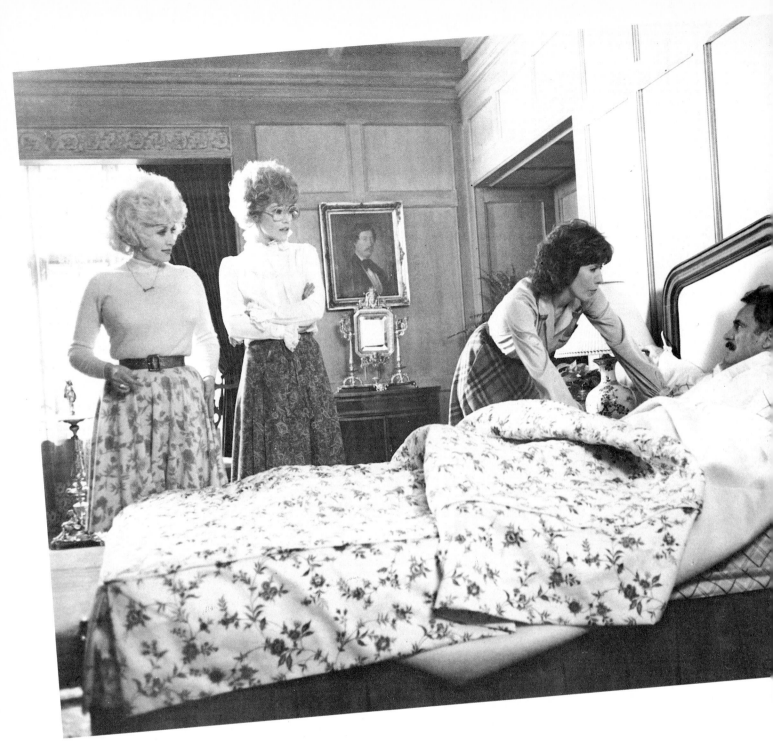

Above : *Women's revenge for generations of male domination found a funny side in* **Nine to Five** *(1980) in which a trio of office workers (Dolly Parton, Jane Fonda and Lily Tomlin) kidnap their chauvinist boss (Dabney Coleman) as a way of getting even.*

Right: *The reclusive but much admired superstar Robert Redford scooped an Oscar for his first (and thus far only) film as director,* **Ordinary People** *(1980), about the emotional anticyclones that cause havoc with a repressed middle-class family. Donald Sutherland and Mary Tyler Moore played the parents; Timothy Hutton won a Best Supporting Actor Oscar as the suicidal son.*

the basic premise of these films — that the endangering of female life is more exciting, both to the criminal and to certain members of the audience, than the endangering of male life — to pin down the tacit sexual titillation of these pictures. But just as by their efforts radical women all but drove off the screen films that offered rape as a voyeuristic spectacle, so they turned their protesting attentions to this cycle of unlovely "women-in-peril" pictures.

Having made colossal gains through a canny awareness of the way they were portrayed by the media, women were understandably not prepared to give an inch. With the exception of the crudest exploitation movies, many films now viewed them with a fresh understanding and respect.

Top : *Dino De Laurentiis spent a fortune updating (1976) the classic* **King Kong** *(1933) for the Seventies and received no praise from the critics, although the ape effects were superior. Former model Jessica Lange proved herself an attractive light comedienne as the Beauty who tames the Beast.*

Right: *Brian De Palma's* **Dressed to Kill** *(1980) was one of the most extreme of the young director's homages to the works of Alfred Hitchcock. The model here was* **Psycho** *(1960) and De Palma cast his wife, Nancy Allen, as the young hooker whose life is endangered because she accidentally stumbles into an elevator in which the killer, mentally disturbed and sexually confused, has just murdered an adulterous wife and mother (Angie Dickinson) with a straight razor.*

Far right: *An unusual science fiction thriller, Donald Cammell's* **Demon Seed** *(1977) casts Julie Christie as a scientist's wife who is captured, assaulted and impregnated by the household computer which manages to activate normally inanimate objects in the home.*

Chapter 6
The Kids
with Beards

Chapter 6

Very few people have the sense of balance to observe who is on the ladder behind them. The studio bosses who were reluctantly acknowledging the erosion of their power in the late Sixties could not for the life of them see where the new tycoons would come from. Certainly not from among the ranks of employees of the banks and conglomerates who were taking over the studios. Surely not the directors? Even after the disappointments of **Torn Curtain** (1966) and **Topaz** (1969), Alfred Hitchcock remained the only director whose name alone would sell a mainstream movie. The graduates of the new-fangled film schools couldn't compete with that! What had they ever achieved, the kids with beards who had learnt the theory of film from the blackboard?

Only an opportunistic employer like Roger Corman, then kingpin producer of exploitation movies for American-International Pictures and therefore always on the look-out for cheap young talent, had hired them. And what had he got? A horror film **Dementia 13** (1963) by the then unknown Francis Coppola and a picture about Depression drifters called **Boxcar Bertha** (1972) by one Martin Scorsese. . . .

The other young directors who later became seminal influences in the Hollywood of the Seventies were stirring in their professional prams around this time, some of them making student films. With the exception of Steven Spielberg and Brian De Palma, they were all graduates of the film schools, organizations that were unjustly reviled by movie Establishment figures who believed that cinema was something that simply was or was not in the blood. Previously, the studios themselves had been the film schools. Now this education was provided in more formal surroundings for a generation that had been weaned upon film and had in part, at least, been shaped by the movies they saw. These young Turks sensed where the studios were losing touch with the audience's emotions and expectations, not with a sociologist's overview but simply because they *were* part of that audience at which the movies were imperfectly aimed. They knew what was wrong with the medium; all they needed was the equipment to carry out the repairs. Film school provided it.

St Francis of the film studios

Foremost amongst these newcomers was Francis Coppola, the group's eldest member and the first to break into movies. By the time he made **The Godfather** in 1972 and earned respectability (which in Hollywood equates with box-office returns) for the young graduates,

Right: *George C Scott made sour Oscar history when he declined his Best Actor award for the title role in* **Patton** *(1970). Franklin J Schaffner's complex study of the "red-blooded" American General was cowritten by Francis Coppola and managed at once to be intimate (the opening speech with Scott posed against a gigantic American flag) and epic in the battle sequences.*

he had worked extensively for Corman, written scripts that included **This Property Is Condemned** (1966) and the Oscar-winning **Patton**, directed three films for Warners (**You're a Big Boy Now** (1967), **Finian's Rainbow** (1968) and **The Rain People** (1969)) and seen the shattering of his cinematic Camelot, the idealistic Zoetrope studio system that he had established in San Francisco, and which was later to be resurrected with no more happy an outcome.

Coppola gave George Lucas his first directing chance (**THX 1138** (1971) was the picture that caused the first financial shutdown of Zoetrope) while Lucas went on to become friend, adviser and finally collaborator (on **Raiders of the Lost Ark** (1981)) of Steven Spielberg. Each had and continues to have his own protégés and the names of Zoetrope, Lucasfilm and Amblin' probably mean as much to students of the Seventies as did Paramount, MGM and Universal to earlier film generations.

By the end of the Seventies the three biggest money-spinners in the history of the cinema were all the work of this group. Lucas's **Star Wars** was the leader, closely followed by its 1980 sequel, **The Empire Strikes Back** (actually directed by Irvin Kershner and doing astoundingly well to achieve this position in so short a period of time)

and then by Steven Spielberg's shark saga, **Jaws**. Yet each director retains his integrity and tempers a seeming box-office invulnerability with an occasional appetite for smaller, more personal films that ignore the recipe for surefire hits. For the erratic and unpredictable Coppola it lies in his Zoetrope output; for Lucas the initial commercial disaster of **THX 1138**; for Spielberg it is **The Sugarland Express** and the expensive failure of **1941** (1979). Yet, when they are on form, the names of these directors guarantee box-office success.

Coppola was assigned to **The Godfather** because of his Italian-American background which was supposed to assuage the expressed sensitivity of the Mafia to seeing Mario Puzo's book filmed. In the event it was a handsomely old-fashioned movie, epic in sweep and stature and modern only in the graphic depiction of the violence of organized crime. Coppola's sequel, **The Godfather Part II** (1974), developed the theme of family and the difficulty of one culture assimilating another. To see the two films edited together in the mammoth television version, for which Coppola again shot extra footage, is to appreciate the breadth and complexity of the director's scheme, even though language and violence had been muted for home consumption.

Far left: *Action in North Africa during World War II in* **Patton** *(1970).*

Left: *A canny cocktail of all the myths and legends that excite the appetites of children,* **Star Wars** *(1977) placed writer- director George Lucas among the giants of cinema commerce. Alec Guinness won an Oscar nomination for his performance as Ben [Obi Wan] Kenobi,*

Below: *A self-consciously innovative debut movie by director George Lucas,* **THX 1138** *(1971). Set in the 25th century, it largely features drugged, shaven-headed characters who are dressed in white and photographed against white backgrounds. Robert Duvall and Donald Pleasence (left) are the enemies in this bleak futuristic society.*

Right: *One of Coppola's best films of the Seventies, critically lauded yet not a crowd-pleaser, was* **The Conversation** *(1974) in which Gene Hackman played an electronics surveillance expert drawn into the lives of the people he is bugging, with disastrous results. But the bugger is himself finally bugged, or so he believes – he wrecks his apartment in searching for the elusive device.*

Bottom right and far right: *An irredeemably juvenile sense of humor blocked the success of* **1941** *(1979) and, despite a huge budget and unstinting effects, provided the first real flop for flavor-of-the-month director Steven Spielberg after* **Jaws** *(1975) and* **Close Encounters of the Third Kind** *(1977). A farcical account of one stray Japanese submarine that surfaces off the Californian coast after Pearl Harbor and the chaos engendered in the local community, it remained as mechanically funny as a penny-in-the-slot laughing sailor in an amusement park. Oblivious of war, meanwhile, a soldier (Treat Williams) and a dishwasher (Bobby DiCicco) settle a dispute over the girl played by Dianne Kay.*

In between the twin parts of this massive project came **The Conversation** (1974), a gripping paranoia thriller that captures the mood of Watergate with its depiction of the breakdown of a man (an excellent performance by Gene Hackman) who works in electronic surveillance as a professional eavesdropper. Thereafter Coppola turned his energies to another epic project, **Apocalypse Now** (1979), which he had prepared in the late Sixties and now realized at great personal cost (the near-collapse of his marriage, the mortgaging of his home as the budget whirlwinded to more than 30 million dollars). Homecoming soldiers had reported that the Vietnam War was like a movie; Coppola's film itself became a war, afflicted by everything from the heart attack of one of the principal actors to the destruction of whole sets by a typhoon. Those who endured and survived the combat zone of **Apocalypse Now** spoke of consuming obsession and near-madness in its making, but the picture is its own justification: a great moral work.

Coppola, not only on account of his prodigious talent but also perhaps because he is the spiritual father of the new generation of film-makers, has always been acknowledged by the movie Establishment. Best Picture Oscars went to both **The Godfather** and **The Godfather Part II**, while **The Conversation** won the top award of the Cannes Film Festival. Ironically, the film-making panache and the commercial Titanism of Lucas and Spielberg have yet to be rewarded by Oscar.

Lucas: music and mythology

George Lucas was helped by Coppola in setting up **American Graffiti**, a rites of passage film made almost unbearably nostalgic by the music of the day (1962), as a group of friends spend their last evening together before going their separate ways to college and adult life. This was almost certainly the most influential film of the early Seventies, much imitated and one to which a young audience quickly responded and flocked in droves. But not in the numbers that queued again and again for Lucas's next film, **Star Wars**.

It was no idle stroke of luck that **Star Wars** became the highest grossing movie in the history of the cinema. George Lucas devoted two years to researching the myths that resoundingly appeal to young audiences the world over. He "created" the film in the most cold-blooded, premeditated way possible. Far from making him rich, his previous two films had left him on the brink of poverty; **Star Wars**, he vowed, would make him a millionaire. He acquired the merchandising rights from the studio (an unprecedented request by a film-maker), conceived his story as part of a trilogy (that was itself part of an even larger plan) and worked hard and imaginatively to bring in an expensive-looking film on a modest budget. The result was a special effects fantasy extravaganza that mixes Arthurian legend with

Top far right: *The droids were two of the big attractions of* **Star Wars** *(1977), anticipating the cute E.T. of five years later. The finicky, faintly camp C-3PO (Anthony Daniels, pictured), a worrier of Woody Allen class, was neatly contrasted with the happy-go-lucky Daleklike R2-D2, played by Kenny Baker.*

Right, below right and bottom:
***Apocalypse Now** (1979)* embroiders on Conrad's original story by having a professional army killer (Martin Sheen) sent to "terminate" Col. Kurtz, who has enlisted local head-hunting tribesmen in an unauthorized sideshow campaign. But the special agent has to assume the persona of his target, now his alter ego, before he can complete the hit.

frontier mythology, and grafts World War II aerial dogfight choreography on to the clinical fantasy of Kubrick's **2001: A Space Odyssey** (a great favorite of Lucas's). It's a junk-food movie in a designer pack; it is low in nutritional value, but it's fast and fun. That Lucas's genuine understanding of the mechanism that made Saturday matinée serials work was not a flash in the pan was demonstrated when he joined forces with Spielberg for their salute to that all-but-forgotten genre in **Raiders of the Lost Ark**.

Spielberg: brat of brilliance

One could argue that Steven Spielberg had no need of film school in that he was a precocious movie brat from his earliest days. With access to a home movie camera, he was making films before his contemporaries were dating girls. Once, according to legend, on a Universal studio tour, he broke away from the main party and joined the "real" world of the working studio. Months later he had worked his way on to the lot where now stands his own architect-designed suite of offices, a thank-you from the people who banked the checks for **E.T. – The Extra-Terrestrial** (1982).

The made-for-television movie **Duel** brought Spielberg to critical attention: remarkable notices for this tale of a traveling salesman followed and menaced by a seemingly driverless truck resulted in the film's opening on the movie circuit, but **The Sugarland Express** disappointed the studio's high commercial hopes. It was nevertheless an outstandingly accomplished first feature film, the tragi-comic story of a prison break and its consequences. But it was with **Jaws** that Spielberg's earning potential finally matched his prodigious talent.

This nightmare rollercoaster ride, a monster movie torn from real life, probably caused a sharp downturn in the numbers of ocean bathers the world over even in the hot summers of 1975 and 1976. (Swimming pool attendances possibly dipped, too, since Spielberg's

movie was plugged in to primal fears of the water and the idea of people as food.) A difficult film to direct on watery locations, it ran over budget and over schedule, but amply justified the investment of time, trust and money. There was suspense to rival that of Hitchcock and a new mechanical star in Bruce, the killer shark. Or, rather, Spielberg demonstrated the importance of the effect, the film itself, as star rather than the chemistry of actors (good as Roy Scheider, Robert Shaw and Richard Dreyfuss were in their roles).

Even so, Spielberg's understanding of tension and suspense meant that he never retreated into the safe haven of effects for their own sake. This could easily have been the case in a film like **Close Encounters of the Third Kind** (the title being quasi-scientific jargon for contact with extra-terrestrials). By far the largest portion of this long film concerns the telepathic awareness of a group of geographically separated people that something of moment is about to occur at a specific location. The way in which the director delays (and thus increases his audience's desire for) his amazing visual climax is exemplary. Even in the "Special Edition" of the film, a version re-cut by Spielberg and released three years later, the emphasis on effects was hardly accentuated. It was, in any case, a film that appealed to spiritual hungers rather than to genre expectations, one that suggested that God was not only alive and well but even planning a visit. And as the little childlike aliens exchange crew with their human hosts at the film's emotionally draining climax, we get our first glimpse of the ancestors of E.T.

Scorsese: realism and redemption

Unlike Lucas and Spielberg, Martin Scorsese has never claimed the cinema of wonder as his constituency. His films are usually

Left: Steven Spielberg's **Duel** (1971) was a made-for-television movie but admiring critics campaigned for its cinema release. Based on a Richard Matheson story about a traveling salesman (Dennis Weaver) menaced with deadly intent by a huge and seemingly driverless truck, the film became a masterly exercise in suspense. It was on the evidence of this success that Spielberg was entrusted with **Jaws** (1975) and set on the mainstream commercial highway.

Above and top: **Close Encounters of the Third Kind** (1977) (scientific jargon for actual contact with extra-terrestrials) was a huge success for Steven Spielberg and for the extra-special effects of Douglas Trumbull. Richard Dreyfuss played an electrical repair man whose initial sighting of alien craft leaves him with a telepathic imprint of the site of the imminent landing. When he gatecrashes the reception party being organized for the vast Mother Ship....

Left: *When the friendly alien Mother Ship finally arrives in* **Close Encounters of the Third Kind** *(1977), we are treated to a magnificent firework display of models and effects, plus our first sight of E.T.'s relatives.*

Below: *Although much of the film was shot in Los Angeles locations, Martin Scorsese's* **Mean Streets** *(1973) offers a wholly convincing view of growing up against the background of gang life in New York's Little Italy. This very personal film, inspired by the director's own experiences and anxieties, starred Harvey Keitel and Robert De Niro who went on to become stalwarts of Scorsese's repertory company of actors. The feckless Johnny Boy (De Niro), running away from mob vengeance with Charlie (Keitel) and his girl (Amy Robinson), is shot in Brooklyn by a hired gun (played by Scorsese himself) and seriously, perhaps fatally, injured.*

passionate, bleak and concerned with redemption, a theme carried over from his religious upbringing (at one point he planned to become a priest). The Italian-American milieu of **Mean Streets** (1973) invited comparison with **The Godfather**, but was more aptly viewed as a preparation for his blisteringly fierce **Taxi Driver**, in which the would-be savior becomes an exterminating angel.

Like the rest of "the kids with beards", Scorsese is a highly cine-literate man who refers to or quotes frequently from the directors he admires and the movies that colored his childhood. Just as **Alice Doesn't Live Here Anymore** opens with the heroine as a child inhabiting the sunset glow of the old Warner Brothers romances of the late Forties and protesting, with anachronistic colorfulness, that she can sing better than 20th Century-Fox's Alice Faye, so **New York, New York**, Scorsese's sober and serious 1977 musical, pounds the same turf as Coppola's **One From the Heart** (1982). Both are highly stylized films and the heightened artificiality of the sets (New York and Las Vegas reconstructed in Los Angeles) pays tribute to the musicals of the years in which the directors were growing up. **New York, New York** has a further dimension in that its plot outline, about a female entertainer's successful rise to fame and the subsequent eclipse of her husband's career, echoes the 1954

version of the classic **A Star Is Born**, in which Judy Garland played the ascendant star. Here her daughter, Liza Minnelli, plays the central role and a big production number, "Happy Endings", mirrors cleverly the classic "Born in a Trunk" production number from the earlier film.

De Palma's nightmare vision

Such quotations could quickly become tedious to a general audience if the films did not add contemporary layers of meaning of their own and entertain even as they imitate (or pay homage). In this regard Scorsese has proved himself a master while another of the young directors, Brian De Palma, has become increasingly introspective. His cinematic obsession with the films of Alfred Hitchcock has lasted from the 1973 **Sisters** to the present day. This was his **Rear Window** (1954) (a murder glimpsed in part from a neighbor's flat); the subsequent **Obsession** (1976) was his **Vertigo** (1958) (a grieving

Left: *Geneviève Bujold had a dual role in Brian De Palma's* **Obsession** *(1975), a homage by the movie-literate director to Alfred Hitchcock's* **Vertigo** *(1958). Bujold played both the kidnapped wife of a wealthy businessman (Cliff Robertson), killed in a botched attempt to catch the villains with fake ransom money, and the lookalike girl he meets in Italy many years later.*

Brian De Palma's handsome shocker **Carrie** (1975), made telling use of split-screen techniques to follow cause and effect as it monitored the startling telekinetic powers of a teenage girl (Sissy Spacek) passing through a traumatic puberty. Cause: the sadistic tyranny of Piper Laurie's religious zealot of a mother. Effect: a fiery whizzbang of a finale in which she fries her tormentors to a crisp and the High School Prom turns into a blazing nightmare.

widower comforted and confounded by the seeming double of his dead wife). These same two Hitchcock models are doubled up in his recent **Body Double**, suggesting that inspiration is now running at low ebb, but De Palma's best work in the Seventies was done off his own bat: the vigorous, pounding rock opera **Phantom of the Paradise** and his big commercial breakthrough film, **Carrie**.

Sissy Spacek was outstanding as the shy, tortured teenage daughter of a religious zealot (Piper Laurie), whose burgeoning adolescent sexuality gives her a hellish time at high school, unleashing a frightening telekinetic power through which she wreaks a fearsome revenge on her tormentors. De Palma revived and developed the old split-screen technique of the Sixties to show us cause and effect simultaneously and, in the process, provide us with one of the most powerful and original horror movies of the decade. **Carrie** was taken from the first novel of the prolific Stephen King and, just as De Palma has never since found such stimulating source material, neither has King found a more ideally suited screen interpreter for his bold writing: the two should reunite.

The striking thing about this group (Coppola, Lucas and Spielberg in particular) is the way in which they split and regroup, move from genre to genre and in some instances from studio to studio, but always maintain a selfless love of movies for their own sake. Just as Coppola's protégé George Lucas has already gone on to outgross him with the **Star Wars** cycle, it is conceivable that a Spielberg alumnus like Robert Zemeckis may yet teach his master a thing or two, now that the commercially quiet start of the Beatles-inspired **I Wanna Hold Your Hand** (1978) and the over-the-top comedy **Used Cars** (1980) (projects underwritten by Spielberg) has given way to such blockbusters as **Romancing the Stone** (1984) and **Back to the Future** (1985).

The kids with beards constantly plow back profits and fame, investing in their own futures and that of the industry. The past, as they have learned from the old studio bosses, has taken care of itself.

Right: In **Carrie** (1975), the bigoted, sex-obsessed mother (Piper Laurie) of a pubescent girl (Sissy Spacek) associates "the curse of Eve" and its attendant blood with sin, death and crucifixion, as well as dangerous female sexuality. In sheer self-defense, her unfortunate child finally "crucifies" her with flying knives, projected by her telekinetic powers.

PICTURE CREDITS

Ronald Grant: 26-27, 37 bottom, 80-81 centre, 98 top left; **Kobal Collection:** 1, 2-3, 6-11, 13-15, 16 top, 17 top, 18-22, 23 top, 25, 28-29 top centre, 29 bottom, 30 top, 32, 33, 34 top, 35, 36, 38-41, 44-45, 47-50, 53, 54 left, 55 top right, 56-57, 59, 60, 61 top, 63 inset, 64 top, 66-67, 70-71, 80 top, 82, 86-87, 88, 88-89, 90-97, 98-99, 102 top left, 104-105, 111 top, 112-113 top, 113 bottom, 114-115 bottom, 116-117; **National Film Archives:** Endpapers, 4-5, 12-13, 16 bottom, 17 bottom, 23 bottom, 24, 28 bottom, 31, 34-35 bottom centre, 37 top, 42-43, 46, 51-52, 54-55 centre, 58, 60-61 bottom centre, 64-65, 68-69, 72-73, 81 bottom right, 83, 84-85, 89 top left, 101, 102-103, 108-109, 110, 112 bottom, 114 top, 118-119; **David Shipman:** 62-63, 100.

Multimedia Publications (UK) Limited have endeavored to observe the legal requirements with regard to the rights of suppliers of photographic material.